MONETIZE
CLOUD & AI

From technology innovation to business excellence

CHU WENCHANG

PARTRIDGE

Library of Congress Control Number: 2024921672
ISBN: Hardcover   978-1-5437-8272-1
                 Softcover   978-1-5437-8273-8
                 eBook   978-1-5437-8271-4

Print information available on the last page.

To order additional copies of this book, contact
Toll Free +65 3165 7531 (Singapore)
Toll Free +60 3 3099 4412 (Malaysia)
orders.singapore@partridgepublishing.com

www.partridgepublishing.com/singapore

PREFACE

Since the first decade of this century, with the rapid development and popularization of cloud computing, more and more technical capabilities have been provided to enterprise and individual developers through the network. Cloud computing services themselves have long exceeded the scope of computing services. Various technical capabilities such as computing, storage, networking, security, communication capabilities, and media services have all been deployed in the cloud and provided to users around the world through the network.

Especially today's booming artificial intelligence products, which can be quickly promoted and used, are also due to the use of the network-provided method, which is essentially a cloud service.

This cloud-based technical service capability has achieved technology inclusiveness, greatly reducing the cost of using advanced technical capabilities for small and medium-sized enterprises, and also greatly accelerating the promotion and popularization of new technical capabilities. Moreover, based on existing cloud capabilities, it has also given birth to the innovation of new technical capabilities. This is an era of technological explosion and an era of accelerated innovation.

However, large-scale and sustainable technological innovation must be aimed at commercial success, because without economic returns, it is difficult to have sustained investment, and without commercial success, it also indicates that this innovation is not an innovation that is widely needed by current society.

Different from consumer goods, the technical service capabilities provided through the network have their particularities when commercialized. Its product structure is significantly different from those of ordinary consumer goods, and its customer journey is longer, which is reflected in product awareness and business interfaces.

In terms of product awareness, the product structure of cloud services is relatively complex, and the pricing structure varies greatly. How to make most customers easily understand these product structures, there are many special considerations in the commercial design of products, and the product capabilities need to be expressed in the way that the customer has the strongest perception of the product value, while hiding the underlying technical structure of the product.

From the perspective of the business interface, since most of the customers of cloud services are enterprises, research institutions, universities, government departments, etc., these customers are not one person, but a group of people, a group of people with different divisions, such as management, technical departments, purchasing departments, and finance departments. Cloud service providers themselves are also composed of multiple departments, so the business interface here is actually a mesh connection of a group of people to another group of people. These people will be responsible for their respective responsibilities at different stages, raise their respective concerns, and form interactions between the two parties. Moreover, most of these interaction actions are completed through the network rather than face-to-face. How to efficiently complete the interaction of different stages in the customer journey on the network is what needs to be structurally designed and implemented when cloud services are commercialized. This is actually the design of the digital business interface between provider-customer.

I have been engaged in the field of digital business operation for nearly twenty years, and deeply feel that the information objects that need to be designed and processed in this field are very complex, and the business processes that need to be supported are also numerous. However, many enterprises, especially technology innovative companies, often focus their talents and energy on the product capabilities themselves, but lack experience in digital business operations, which often hinders these companies from growing rapidly and on a large scale, and also results in a relatively poor purchase and use experience for their customers, which is actually a pity.

Regardless of the type of cloud-based technical capability, when it is commercialized and enters the market, there are actually many commonalities in the business processes that need to be followed and the areas that need special attention. This is actually an e-commerce market dedicated to selling cloud services. Therefore, I summarize my experiences and provide a methodology for the commercialization of technical service capabilities, and compiles it into this book, hoping to provide an effective commercialization path for more technology innovative companies, especially those that provide cloud-based technology innovative products through the network, and realize the path from technological innovation to business success.

Chu Wenchang
October 17th 2024, Singapore

CONTENTS

1 Monetization for Technologies 1

  1.1 General Process for Monetization 1
  1.2 Commerce System for Monetization 7

2 Product 12

  2.1 Product Attributes 13
  2.2 Geographical Relevance 14
    2.2.1 Vast Number of Product Specifications 16
    2.2.2 Continuous Iteration and Evolution 21
  2.3 Pricing Model 23
    2.3.1 PAYG Pricing 25
    2.3.2 Subscription-Based Pricing 26
    2.3.3 Floor-Ceiling Pricing 27
    2.3.4 "Saving Plan" Pricing 30
  2.4 Product Presentation 32
    2.4.1 Functional Features 34
    2.4.2 Pricing Introduction 36
    2.4.3 Interactive Demo 38
    2.4.4 Case Study 39
    2.4.5 Product Catalogue 42
    2.4.6 Product Portfolio 43
  2.5 GTM Strategy 44
    2.5.1 Positioning & Proposition 44
    2.5.2 Seed Customer 48
    2.5.3 Distribution Channel 50
  2.6 Product Performance 53
    2.6.1 Product Experience 54
    2.6.2 Product Cost 57
    2.6.3 Product Profit 59
    2.6.4 Product Problem 61
  2.7 Product Lifecycle 63
    2.7.1 Fail Fast 65
    2.7.2 BCG Matrix 67

2.7.3 Product Retirement...70
2.7.4 Total Lifetime Value...71

3 Customer 73

3.1 Customer Acquisition..73
3.1.1 Customer Segmentation 75
3.1.2 Content Marketing..78
3.1.3 Freemium Strategy 82
3.1.4 Customer Nurturing 84
3.2 Customer Onboarding 86
3.2.1 Customer Account..88
3.2.2 Customer Verification 91
3.2.3 Customer Organization 93
3.3 Customer Communication....................................94
3.3.1 Digital Channel...98
3.3.2 Communication History.................................100
3.3.3 Personalize Communication 103
3.4 Loyalty and Retention..105
3.4.1 Customer Loyalty 107
3.4.2 Customer Retention......................................110
3.4.3 Customer Retirement....................................113
3.4.4 Customer Lifetime Value...............................115

4 Ordering 117

4.1 Order Configuration 120
4.1.1 Configuration vs Scenario 122
4.1.2 Availability Check..122
4.1.3 Pricing Display 125
4.1.4 Product Recommendations 127
4.2 Shopping Cart..128
4.2.1 Good shopping cart 129
4.2.2 Compatibility Check 131
4.3 Order Payment...132
4.3.1 Payment Method 134
4.3.2 Payment Security..136
4.3.3 Anti Money Laundering 138
4.4 Provisioning and Deployment............................141

4.4.1 Provisioning Orchestration 143
4.4.2 Activating AI Product...............................145
4.5 Subscription Management...............................146
4.5.1 Subscription Modification 147
4.5.2 Subscription Renewal...............................150
4.5.3 Subscription Cancellation 152

5 Billing...............................155

5.1 Usage Metering...............................158
5.1.1 Critical Role in Cloud Business...............................159
5.1.2 Typical Types of Cloud Metering...............................161
5.1.3 Typical Types of AI Product Metering...............................164
5.1.4 AI Powered Metering 166
5.2 Usage Rating 168
5.2.1 Rating Factors 169
5.2.2 Rating Engine 170
5.2.3 Estimated Rating...............................172
5.3 Bill & Invoice...............................174
5.3.1 Billing Cycle 175
5.3.2 Bill Generation 176
5.3.3 Bill Splitting 177
5.4 Billing Experience...............................179
5.4.1 Bill Statement...............................181
5.4.2 Billing Communication 184
5.4.2 Bill Dispute 186
5.5 Cost Optimization 188
5.5.1 Unnecessity Identification...............................189
5.5.2 Right-Size the Service...............................190
5.6 Revenue Assurance...............................192
5.6.1 Anomaly Detection...............................193
5.6.2 Billing Reconciliation...............................195
5.6.3 AI for Assurance...............................196

6 Sales 198

6.1 Sales Pipeline 199
6.1.1 Lead 200
6.1.2 Opportunity 205

6.1.3 Sales Closure Analysis 207
6.1.4 Sales Forecasting....................................209
6.2 CPQ..211
6.2.1 Configuration.....................................212
6.2.2 Pricing 214
6.2.3 Quotation 216
6.2.4 Guided Selling..................................217
6.3 Sales Promotion 220
6.3.1 Discounts 223
6.3.2 Coupons...224
6.3.3 Rebates 226
6.3.4 Points-based system 227
6.4 Agreement 229
6.4.1 Enterprise Agreement.......................231
6.4.2 Subscription Agreement....................235
6.4.3 Agreement Fulfillment......................237

7 Partner 240

7.1 Product Partner..241
7.1.1 Partner Model 242
7.1.2 Product Information.........................245
7.1.3 Offer Integrating 247
7.1.4 Revenue Settlement 248
7.1.5 Cloud Marketplace 250
7.2 Sales Partner..251
7.2.1 Reseller & Distributor 254
7.2.2 Recruitment & Onboarding 257
7.2.3 Incentive Programs 261
7.2.4 Renewal & Termination....................264
7.3 Service Partner...268
7.3.1 Solution Consulting Partner 270
7.3.2 Managed Service Partner 271
7.3.3 Service as Sales 274

8 Business Excellence in Technology Industry....................278

1

MONETIZATION FOR TECHNOLOGIES

1.1 General Process for Monetization

If you're interested in how to introduce an advanced technology product to the market and attain commercial success, if your company is grappling with complex business processes and achieving less than anticipated results, or if you're concerned about the inefficient operational processes of a tech firm, then congratulations, you've discovered the book you require.

This book aims to describe the methodologies and practices for monetizing cloud and AI products.

Product monetization refers to the process of generating revenue from a product or service. It involves converting the value created by the product or service into financial returns for the business. In the context of cloud computing and AI industry, product monetization specifically refers to the strategies and methods used by Cloud Service Providers (CSPs) or AI service Providers to generate revenue from the cloud-based services they offer to customers.

Currently, there are hundreds of companies offering various forms of cloud services, including major tech giants, cloud service providers, small startups, and enterprises from various industries.

Properly designing and packaging cloud-enabled technology products for monetization, as well as efficiently and rapidly promoting them to global markets, is a crucial topic for technology companies.

Although the monetization of technology products shares some similarities with traditional products, it also possesses unique characteristics and requirements due to the nature of cloud-based technology. Providers need to clearly communicate the value propositions and solutions of the technology product, enabling clients to understand how it addresses their business needs and adds value. Meanwhile, providers need to offer a convenient and smooth product ordering, usage, and billing experience, allowing customers and users to efficiently manage their usage costs of technological products.

Thus, the product monetization will extend and encompass the domains **of Product, Customer, Ordering, Billing, Sales, and Partner.** This means that it will cover not only the basic aspects of these domains but also dive deeper into their interrelationships and the potential for generating revenue from each.

- **Product**

The product is the core of the cloud business, as the features, functionality, and value created by the provider are conveyed through the product to the customer. Designing an effective product management mechanism is crucial for effectively conveying all relevant information from the product team to the marketing team, sales team, service team, and, most importantly, the customer.

For cloud service products, the product is the lifeblood of its commercial operations. The completeness of product information determines the overall health of the business operations. This means that if the product information is incomplete or inaccurate, it may cause operational issues in sales, marketing, customer service, and other areas, ultimately impacting the success of the business. Therefore, ensuring the comprehensiveness and accuracy of product information is crucial for maintaining smooth business operations. This includes conveying all aspects of the product, such as its features, characteristics, pricing, and value propositions, effectively across all relevant teams to ensure that the end customer can fully understand and appreciate the product's value.

- **Customer**

Customers are the goal of business success, and the company's understanding and reach of its customers determine whether it can achieve this goal. This book will provide a detailed description of the entire process of customer acquisition, onboarding, communication, and retention.

It covers not only how to effectively identify and attract potential customers but also how to provide new customers with a seamless onboarding experience to ensure they transition smoothly to using the company's products and services. Additionally, this book explores ongoing customer communication strategies, how to establish and maintain strong customer relationships, and best practices to enhance customer satisfaction and loyalty. Through these systematic strategies and methods, businesses can significantly improve customer retention rates, maximize customer lifetime value, and achieve lasting business success.

- **Ordering**

For Cloud Service Providers (CSPs), the most exciting moment is when customers start placing orders to purchase products.

Providing a smooth product ordering experience and ensuring that customers can quickly access and start using the necessary product features is a core aspect of efficient commercial operations.

To achieve this goal, CSPs need to design a simple and intuitive ordering process, reducing complexity and barriers for customers during the selection and purchase process.

Additionally, CSPs should offer comprehensive support and guidance to help customers quickly understand and utilize the products they have purchased. This includes providing detailed product documentation, online training, real-time customer support, and continuous technical updates and improvements. Through these measures, CSPs can not only enhance customer satisfaction but also promote higher customer retention and repurchase rates, thereby driving sustainable business growth.

- **Billing**

Unlike consumer products is pre-paid, most cloud products are post-paid.

Customers can scale their usage flexibly according to their needs, and after a certain usage period, the CSP sends a bill based on the actual usage. Therefore, the accuracy and clarity of the bill are crucial for customers.

To ensure that customers accurately understand their usage and cost structure, CSPs need to provide transparent and detailed billing information. The bill should include the specific usage of each service, the pricing standards, the discount given, and the total cost, clearly categorizing and explaining the source of each charge.

This book will provide a detailed explanation of the methods and processes about how to effectively gather and record customer usage data, ensure the accuracy and timeliness of billing, and generate clear and understandable bills and invoices.

Additionally, the book will explore various revenue assurance measures to ensure that the enterprise's earnings are fully protected and to minimize customer churn due to billing issues. Through these comprehensive methods and processes, enterprises can optimize their financial management, improve customer satisfaction, and promote stable business growth.

- **Sales**

The theories and methods of sales have been extensively described in numerous books available in the market, and there are many tools that can automate the sales process. However, this book focuses on the unique characteristics of selling cloud products. This includes the processes of configuring, quoting, and contracting for complex cloud products, as well as effective promotional methods.

Selling cloud products presents unique challenges and opportunities. Since cloud products are often highly customizable and have complex feature combinations, sales personnel need to deeply understand the specific needs of customers and be able to correctly configure products to meet those needs. This process involves using advanced configuration, pricing, and quoting (CPQ) tools to provide each customer with a personalized solution and quotation.

Additionally, this book will explore how to use data-driven promotional strategies to attract new customers and retain existing ones. Effective promotional methods may include limited-time discounts, free trials, bundled sales, and usage-based pricing models. Through these strategies, sales teams can better demonstrate the value of cloud products, increasing customers' willingness to purchase and their loyalty.

By analyzing these unique sales characteristics and strategies in detail, this book will provide practical guidance for sales teams, helping them achieve success in a competitive market. Businesses can use these methods to optimize their sales processes, improve sales efficiency, and ultimately achieve business growth and market expansion.

■ **Partner**

Today, the development of any industry relies on its ecosystem. This is especially true in the cloud computing industry, where no single company can meet all customer needs across product delivery, sales, and service. Therefore, collaborating with partners to expand product variety, broaden sales channels, and enhance service capabilities is a common and necessary strategy.

This book will provide a detailed description of how Cloud Service Providers (CSPs) can develop and manage more suitable partners.

Developing the proper partners requires CSPs to have a clear partner strategies and value propositions in place, demonstrating the mutual benefits to partner.

CSPs need to identify the core competencies and market coverage of potential partners and attract these partners to their ecosystem by offering technical support, training, and market resources.

Additionally, CSPs should develop flexible partnership models and incentive mechanisms through partner programs to ensure that partners can find suitable roles and positions within the ecosystem.

Managing partners requires establishing an effective partner relationship management system. CSPs should regularly communicate and collaborate with partners, understand their needs, and feedback, and provide support and assistance when necessary. By establishing transparent collaboration processes and clear performance evaluation standards, CSPs can ensure that partners operate efficiently in their respective fields and achieve common business goals.

1.2 Commerce System for Monetization

To manage products, customers, orders, billing, sales and partners better, service providers need to build or purchase a complete set of IT systems to automate these business processes and manage related business data. This system is what we call the Commerce System of CSP for monetization.

A commerce system facilitates the buying, selling, and provisioning of cloud-based products and services. It serves as a central hub for managing transactions, subscriptions, billing, and provisioning across various cloud offerings.

A commerce system for cloud services plays a critical role in facilitating commerce transactions, enabling revenue growth, and enhancing the customer experience in the cloud marketplace ecosystem. It provides the infrastructure and tools needed to monetize cloud offerings, streamline business operations, and drive business success in the digital economy.

When it comes to commerce systems, people are more familiar with the one for the retail industries. However, cloud services, as a type of technical commodity, have their own unique characteristics.

Cloud commerce systems and retail commerce systems serve different purposes and cater to different types of businesses. Here are some key differences between the two:

1. **Nature of Products**:

    - **Cloud Commerce System**: Designed for selling digital products and services that are delivered over the internet, such as software-as-a-service (SaaS), platform-as-a-service (PaaS), or infrastructure-as-a-service (IaaS) offerings. These products are typically subscription-based or usage-based and may require provisioning and deployment in a cloud environment.

It should be noted that as an emerging technology, AI products are also provided through the internet, so they can be regarded as a type of cloud service in terms of monetization.

- **Retail Commerce System**: Designed for selling physical goods or tangible products, such as clothing, electronics, appliances, or groceries, through brick-and-mortar stores, online stores, or both. These products are typically shipped to customers or purchased in-store.

2. Delivery Method:

- **Cloud Commerce System**: Products and services are delivered digitally over the internet, often through cloud-based platforms or applications. Customers access and use these products remotely, typically through web browsers or dedicated software clients.

- **Retail Commerce System**: Products are physically shipped to customers' addresses or picked up in-store. Transactions may occur online or in-person, depending on the retailer's business model and distribution channels.

3. Billing and Pricing Models:

- **Cloud Commerce System**: Typically employs subscription-based, usage-based, or pay-as-you-go pricing models for cloud services. Billing is often automated and based on resource consumption, usage metrics, or predetermined subscription plans.

- **Retail Commerce System**: Uses traditional pricing models such as fixed prices, or volume-based pricing for physical products. Billing may involve tax calculations, shipping fees, and payment processing for each transaction.

4. **Integration with Cloud Services**:

- **Cloud Commerce System**: Integrates with cloud service providers' APIs and platforms to automate provisioning, deployment, billing, and management of cloud resources and services. Requires seamless interoperability with various cloud environments and APIs.

- **Retail Commerce System**: May integrate with third-party systems such as inventory management, point-of-sale (POS), and customer relationship management (CRM) systems. Focuses on managing physical inventory, orders, shipments, and in-store transactions.

Despite its own characters, Commerce system for cloud service still shares the same functionality framework with the one for traditional retail industries:

1. **Product Catalog Management:** Allows businesses to create, manage, and organize their products or services within the system. This includes defining product attributes, categories, pricing, and availability.

2. **Order Management:** Handles the entire order lifecycle, from order creation to fulfillment and delivery. This includes order processing, inventory management, shipping, and returns.

3. **Customer Management:** Manages customer information, profiles, preferences, and interactions. It includes functionalities for customer registration, authentication, segmentation, and personalized experiences.

4. **Payment Processing:** Facilitates secure and efficient payment transactions. This involves integrating with payment gateways, managing payment methods, processing payments, and handling refunds.

5. **Billing and Invoicing:** Manages billing cycles, invoicing, and revenue recognition. It includes functionalities for generating invoices, tracking payments, managing subscriptions, and handling billing disputes.

6. **Promotions and Discounts:** Allows businesses to create and manage promotional campaigns, discounts, coupons, and loyalty programs. It includes functionalities for applying discounts, tracking promotions, and analyzing campaign performance.

7. **Analytics and Reporting:** Provides insights into sales performance, customer behavior, inventory levels, and other key metrics. It includes functionalities for generating reports, dashboards, and analytics tools for data visualization and analysis.

Apart from those functionality features, system also need to provide non-functional features to meet business and management requirements:

1. **Compliance and Security:** Ensures compliance with regulatory requirements and industry standards, such as GDPR, PCI DSS, and SOC2. It includes functionalities for data security, access controls, encryption, and audit trails.

2. **User Experience and Interface:** Provides intuitive and user-friendly interfaces for both administrators and end-users. It includes functionalities for search, navigation, personalization, and responsive design for different devices and screen sizes.

3. **Localization and Globalization:** Supports multiple languages, currencies, and regions to cater to a global customer base. It includes functionalities for localization, translation, and regionalization of content and pricing.

4. **Scalability and Performance:** Ensures the system can handle growing volumes of users, transactions, and data. It includes functionalities for scalability, load balancing, caching, and performance optimization.

The commerce platform plays a pivotal role in driving revenue growth for CSP(Cloud Service Provider)s by facilitating upselling, cross-selling, and renewal opportunities. It enables targeted marketing campaigns, promotions, and personalized recommendations to enhance customer engagement and maximize revenue generation.

Meanwhile, a well-designed commerce platform enhances the overall customer experience by providing intuitive navigation, personalized recommendations, and seamless transaction processes. It reduces friction in the buying journey, increases customer satisfaction, and fosters long-term loyalty and retention.

Overall, the commerce platform serves as a vital infrastructure component in the cloud services ecosystem, enabling CSPs to monetize their offerings, streamline business operations, and deliver value to customers in a dynamic and competitive marketplace.

This book will comprehensively discuss how to build such a Commerce system from various perspectives such as fundamental concepts, advanced methods, and practical experiences. It will delve into the details of each aspect, providing in-depth analysis and practical guidance. By exploring these different perspectives, readers will gain a comprehensive understanding of the complex process of building a successful Commerce system.

2

PRODUCT

Product catalogue management plays a crucial role in shaping the success of cloud services by overseeing the entire lifecycle of products offered in the cloud environment. It involves the organization, maintenance, and presentation of the various products and services offered by a cloud service provider.

The product catalogue serves as a centralized repository for all the cloud-based products and services offered by the provider. It provides a comprehensive view of the available offerings, making it easier for customers to browse and select the solutions that best fit their needs.

For cloud product service providers, products are the core objects of their business, driving key business processes such as sales and service. Whether or not a unified product management system and mechanism can be established is crucial for achieving efficient collaborative development and providing a friendly customer experience.

The cloud service's product management system can be seen as the core intersection connecting the production and sales ends, as it encompasses the entire lifecycle management and operational process of cloud service products.

Each product or service listing in the catalogue includes detailed information such as features, specifications, pricing, availability, and any special terms or conditions. This ensures that customers have access to all the relevant information they need to make informed decisions.

The catalogue management system also should allow for the dynamic updating of product information to reflect changes in offerings, pricing, or availability in real-time. This ensures that customers always have access to the latest and most accurate information.

The product catalogue is tightly integrated with billing and provisioning systems to ensure seamless order processing, billing, and provisioning of services. This integration streamlines the entire customer lifecycle, from selection to deployment to payment.

For global cloud service providers, the product catalogue may support multilingual content to cater to customers in different regions and languages. This enhances accessibility and usability for a diverse customer base.

2.1 Product Attributes

Managing product attributes for cloud services involves defining, organizing, and maintaining the various characteristics and properties that describe the features, functionalities, and specifications of the cloud-based products and services offered by a provider.

Cloud products typically refer to services or solutions delivered over the internet, often through a subscription-based or pay-as-you-go model. These products are intangible and accessed remotely, offering scalable resources and functionalities hosted in cloud infrastructure, while traditional products are tangible goods or physical items that are manufactured, stored, and distributed through physical channels such as retail stores or warehouses. These products have physical attributes such as size, weight, material, and color etc.

Cloud products often offer customization and configuration options that allow customers to tailor the service to their specific needs. Customers can adjust settings, select features, and scale resources dynamically to accommodate changing requirements, while traditional products may have limited customization options, with customers choosing from predefined configurations or specifications. Customization may involve additional costs or lead times, depending on the complexity of the product.

Therefore, the method to describe and manage attribute of Cloud Products is different with what applied on traditional products. It's important to pay attention to the following unique aspects for cloud products:

- o **Geographical relevance**
- o **Vast number of specifications**
- o **Continuous iteration and evolution**

2.2 Geographical Relevance

The geographical relevance of cloud products refers to how the physical location of cloud resources impacts the delivery, performance, and compliance of those services. It encompasses factors such as the location of data centers, network latency, regulatory requirements, and data sovereignty.

Geographical relevance is crucial for several reasons:

1. **Data Sovereignty:** Some regulations require data to be stored within specific jurisdictions. The geographical location of cloud data centers must comply with these regulations to ensure data sovereignty and legal compliance.

2. **Latency and Performance:** The proximity of cloud data centers to end-users affects latency and performance. Placing data centers closer to users reduces latency, resulting in faster response times and better user experience.

3. **Disaster Recovery:** Geographically dispersed data centers provide redundancy and resilience. In the event of a disaster

or outage in one region, services can failover to another region, ensuring business continuity and data availability.

4. **Compliance:** Different regions have varying regulatory requirements regarding data protection, privacy, and security. Compliance with these regulations often necessitates storing data within specific geographical boundaries.

5. **Cost Optimization:** Optimizing the geographical distribution of cloud resources can help reduce costs by leveraging regions with lower energy, labor, or tax expenses. Strategic placement of data centers can lead to cost savings without compromising performance or compliance.

Therefore, when describing the features of cloud products, it's important to consider geographical location as a significant dimension that impacts product functionality, pricing, sales, and provisioning.

To facilitate user identification and selection of various regions within the same cloud service provider (CSP), as well as to improve internal management efficiency, it is recommended to adopt a standardized set of region description IDs and names within the CSP.

Here is a suggested data structure for describing standard region description IDs and names:

```json
{
    "csp_name": "Cloud Provider X",
    "regions": [
        {
            "region_id": "us-east-1",
            "region_name": "US East (Virginia)"
        },
        {
            "region_id": "eu-west-1",
            "region_name": "EU West (Ireland)"
        },
        {
            "region_id": "ap-southeast-1",
            "region_name": "Asia Pacific (Singapore)"
        }
    ]
}
```

In this JSON structure:

- **csp_name** denotes the name of the cloud service provider.
- **regions** is an array containing information about each region.
- Each region object includes the following attributes:
- **region_id**: The standardized region description ID used to uniquely identify the region.
- **region_name**: The standardized name of the region, describing its geographical location or features.

By using such standardized region description IDs and names, it becomes easier for users to identify and select different regions, while also promoting consistency and efficiency in internal management processes.

2.2.1 Vast Number of Product Specifications

The virtual nature of cloud products brings flexibility and scalability, but also results in a vast array of specifications, as they need to cater to diverse users, applications, and scenario requirements.

Take cloud compute product as example, different applications and workloads may require varying specifications of compute resources, such as different numbers of CPU cores, memory capacities, and computational capabilities.

In some major cloud service providers such as Amazon AWS, Microsoft Azure, Google Cloud, they may offer hundreds or even thousands of different specifications of virtual machines. These specifications may be categorized and combined based on factors such as CPU model, memory size, storage type, and network performance to meet the diverse needs of different users and applications.

Additionally, these virtual machine specifications may also include other additional features and characteristics such as GPU acceleration, dedicated hosts, etc., to meet specific user needs and scenarios.

Due to the vast number of specifications of cloud products, cloud providers face the following challenges:

1. **Complexity of Resource Management**: Managing a large numbers of cloud product specifications requires cloud providers to establish sophisticated resource management systems to ensure efficient allocation and utilization of resources.

2. **Customer Segmentation and Service Differentiation**: Cloud providers need to offer cloud products with different specifications to different customer segments and differentiate their services in terms of features, performance metrics, and pricing to meet the diverse needs and budgets of different customers.

3. **Technical Support and Service Level**: Faced with a wide range of cloud product specifications, cloud providers need to provide high-quality technical support and services to help

customers choose and use products that suit their needs and address any issues or challenges that may arise.

4. **Cost Management and Profitability**: Cloud providers need to balance resource investment and profitability to ensure competitiveness and profitability while providing diverse product specifications.

In order to address the aforementioned challenges, a standardized data model becomes essential for expressing and managing the vast number of cloud product specifications. This data model must be applicable across different types of cloud products, such as elastic computing, cloud storage, cloud network and AI product etc.

This standardized data model should:

1. **Capture Diverse Specifications**: It should be capable of capturing diverse specifications related to computing resources, storage options, networking configurations, and other relevant attributes across various types of cloud products.

2. **Support Flexibility and Scalability**: The data model should be flexible and scalable to accommodate new specifications and changes in existing ones over time, reflecting the dynamic nature of cloud environments.

3. **Enable Interoperability**: It should facilitate interoperability between different cloud services and providers, allowing seamless integration and communication between various components and services.

4. **Facilitate Resource Management**: The data model should enable efficient resource management by providing clear representations of resource allocation, utilization, and performance metrics across different specifications.

5. **Support Customer Customization**: The data model should allow for customization to meet specific customer requirements and preferences, enabling personalized configurations while maintaining consistency and coherence.

Overall, a standardized data model serves as a foundation for effectively managing the vast array of cloud product specifications. By providing a common framework for expressing and managing specifications, it helps streamline operations, improve interoperability, and enhance overall efficiency and effectiveness in cloud environments.

SKU (Stock Keeping Unit) is a typical method for identifying and managing product specifications. Although SKU originally comes from the traditional retail industry, its unique ability to provide a clear and unique identifier for product specifications enables it to be effectively utilized throughout the entire product lifecycle, including design, production, sales, after-sales service, and financial settlement, making it a simple and effective method.

An example of a SKU for a cloud product could be:

SKU: CSP-VM-2CPU-8GB-SSD-1Y

In this example:

- "CSP" represents the abbreviation for the cloud service provider.

- "VM" indicates that the SKU is for a virtual machine.

- "2CPU" specifies that the virtual machine has 2 CPU cores.

- "8GB" denotes that the virtual machine has 8 gigabytes of RAM.

- "SSD" indicates that the virtual machine uses SSD storage.

- "1Y" signifies that the SKU is valid for one year.

This SKU provides specific information about the virtual machine's configuration and duration, allowing customers to easily identify and purchase the appropriate cloud product.

In cloud product management, SKU is significant for the following aspects:

1. **Product Identification and Classification**: SKU allows cloud service providers to classify and identify their products, enabling better organization and management of product inventory. By assigning a unique SKU to each product specification, it ensures clear identification of products in management systems, thereby improving management efficiency.

2. **Order Processing and Supply Chain Management**: SKU simplifies the order processing and supply chain management processes. Customers can use SKU to accurately specify the desired product specifications, while suppliers can easily track and manage the various specifications in orders.

3. **Sales and Marketing**: SKU provides convenience for sales and marketing. Sales teams can use SKU to accurately describe and promote various product specifications, providing personalized solutions for customers. Additionally, SKU can be used for pricing strategies and promotional activities to increase product sales and market share.

4. **After-Sales Service and Support**: SKU also plays a role in after-sales service and support. The after-sales team can use SKU to quickly identify customers' product configurations

and provide customized support and solutions. Additionally, SKU can be used for handling product warranties and maintenance services.

2.2.2 Continuous Iteration and Evolution

Due to the ongoing process of refining, enhancing, and updating cloud services to meet the changing needs and demands of users, as well as to incorporate technological advancements and market trends, continuous iteration and evolution of cloud products happens every day.

This iterative approach ensures that cloud products remain competitive, relevant, and aligned with customer expectations over time, but at the same time, it introduces several management challenges for cloud service providers:

1. **Backward Compatibility**: Ensuring that the introduction of new features does not disrupt existing customers' user experience or system integration. New features should be compatible with existing functionalities and should not cause the failure or conflict of current features.

   Cloud providers must ensure the continued availability of old feature functionalities while offering new feature capabilities, as well as ensuring customers can continue to renew their subscriptions.

2. **Customer Communication and Education**: Keeping customers informed about changes, updates, and new features requires effective communication strategies. Cloud service providers must ensure clear and timely communication through various channels, such as release notes, documentation updates, webinars, and support forums. Additionally, educating customers about new features and

best practices helps maximize the value they derive from the cloud products.

3. **Coordination of Cross-Functional Teams**: Continuous iteration involves collaboration between various teams, including development, operations, marketing, and support team. Coordinating these cross-functional teams to ensure seamless communication, alignment of priorities, and efficient workflow can be complex, particularly in large organizations with distributed teams.

Implementing a multi-version strategy for cloud product specifications allows customers and sales teams, under the terms of licensing agreements, to select, purchase, and utilize historical versions of product specifications.

Here's how to address this challenge:

1. **Versioning and Management:** Establish a versioning system for product specifications, ensuring clear identification and management of different versions. Maintain a repository of historical versions, including documentation and release notes detailing changes and updates.

2. **Customer Choice and Selection:** Provide customers with the option to choose from available historical versions of product specifications when making purchases or subscriptions. Offer clear visibility and transparency regarding the differences between versions to enable informed decision-making.

3. **Sales Enablement:** Equip sales teams with the necessary tools and resources to effectively communicate the availability of historical versions to customers. Provide training and guidelines on how to assist customers in selecting the

appropriate version based on their specific requirements and preferences.

4. **Licensing and Compliance:** Ensure that the licensing agreements and terms of use clearly define the rights and permissions associated with accessing and utilizing historical versions of product specifications. Maintain compliance with legal and regulatory requirements governing versioning and licensing.

5. **Support and Maintenance:** Offer support and maintenance services for historical versions of product specifications, ensuring continued reliability and performance. Address any issues or concerns raised by customers using older versions and provide assistance as needed.

6. **Feedback and Improvement:** Gather feedback from customers using historical versions to identify areas for improvement or features that may be missing. Incorporate customer feedback into future updates and iterations of product specifications to enhance overall customer satisfaction.

By implementing a **multi-version strategy** for cloud product specifications and addressing the needs of customers and sales teams, cloud providers can effectively cater to diverse requirements and preferences while maintaining compliance with licensing agreements and regulations.

2.3 Pricing Model

The pricing model for cloud products and services varies depending on factors such as the type of service, usage patterns, customer requirements, and competitive landscape.

A well-designed pricing model can differentiate a CSP from its competitors. It can attract customers by offering better value for money, more flexibility, or innovative pricing structures that meet specific customer needs.

Therefore, pricing model directly impacts a CSP's revenue stream. By setting prices appropriately, CSPs can maximize revenue while remaining competitive in the market. A pricing model that aligns with customer value perception can lead to increased sales and profitability.

Meanwhile, Pricing models help CSPs cover their costs associated with providing cloud services, including infrastructure, maintenance, support, and innovation. Effective pricing ensures that costs are adequately covered while maintaining affordability for customers.

Different pricing models incentivize different usage patterns, which can help CSPs optimize resource allocation and utilization. For example, tiered pricing encourages customers to use resources more efficiently, while spot instances allow CSPs to monetize excessive capacity.

Furthermore, transparent and fair pricing models contribute to customer satisfaction. Customers appreciate clarity and predictability in pricing, as well as the ability to choose pricing plans that best fit their needs and budget. Complex or unpredictable pricing can lead to dissatisfaction and churn.

A strategic pricing model supports long-term growth objectives. It can foster customer loyalty, encourage upselling and cross-selling opportunities, and facilitate expansion into new markets or customer segments.

Overall, the pricing model plays a pivotal role in shaping a CSP's business strategy, revenue generation, customer satisfaction, and competitive positioning in the dynamic cloud computing market. It requires careful consideration, analysis, and refinement to ensure alignment with business objectives and customer needs.

In this section, we aim to introduce readers to several typical pricing models for cloud products, helping them better understand the pricing structures and business models in the cloud service market.

2.3.1 PAYG Pricing

PAYG stands for "Pay-As-You-Go," and it's a pricing model commonly used in cloud computing services. In this model, customers are charged based on their actual usage of the cloud services, rather than a fixed monthly or yearly subscription fee.

The PAYG pricing model has the following characteristics:

1. **Usage-Based Billing:** PAYG allows customers to pay based on their actual usage, rather than prepaying fixed fees. They only pay for the resources they actually use, avoiding unnecessary waste.

2. **Flexibility:** Customers can increase or decrease their usage of resources at any time according to their needs, enabling flexible scaling up and down. This flexibility allows customers to better respond to changes in business requirements.

3. **Granular Billing:** The PAYG model typically bills customers in smaller units, such as hours or minutes, even seconds, enabling them to accurately track their resource usage and adjust as needed.

4. **No Fixed Contracts:** PAYG usually does not require customers to sign long-term contracts or prepay fees. Customers can use cloud services as needed without being tied to contract terms.

5. **Transparency:** The PAYG model often provides a transparent billing structure, allowing customers to clearly understand their costs. This transparency helps customers better predict and control costs.

6. **Suitable for Businesses of All Sizes:** The PAYG model is suitable for businesses of all sizes, from startups to large enterprises. Regardless of the size of the enterprise, they can flexibly use cloud services according to their actual needs, without being restricted by fixed pricing plans.

Overall, the PAYG pricing model provides customers with flexibility, cost-effectiveness, and transparency, enabling them to better manage and optimize their use of cloud resources.

2.3.2 Subscription-Based Pricing

Subscription-based pricing is a pricing model where customers pay a recurring fee at regular intervals (such as monthly or annually) to access a product or service. Here are some key characteristics of subscription-based pricing:

1. **Recurring Fees:** Customers pay a fixed fee on a regular basis, typically monthly or annually, to access the product or service. This fee may remain constant or vary depending on the subscription tier or features chosen.

2. **Access to Services:** Subscribers gain access to the product or service for the duration of their subscription period. This can include access to software applications, digital content, online services, or other resources.

3. **Tiered Pricing:** Subscription-based pricing often offers different subscription tiers or plans with varying features,

capabilities, and price points. Customers can choose the tier that best suits their needs and budget.

4. **Automatic Renewal:** Subscriptions often renew automatically at the end of each billing period unless the customer cancels or changes their subscription. This ensures continuous access to the product or service without interruption.

5. **Scalability:** Subscription-based pricing can offer scalability, allowing customers to easily upgrade or downgrade their subscription plans as their needs change. This flexibility enables customers to adjust their subscription level to match their evolving requirements.

6. **Predictable Costs:** Subscribers benefit from predictable costs, as they know in advance how much they will be charged at each billing cycle. This can help with budgeting and financial planning for individuals and businesses alike.

Subscription-based pricing is commonly used for various products and services, including software-as-a-service (SaaS), streaming media, online publications, and membership-based platform.

It provides a predictable revenue stream for providers and ongoing value for subscribers who continue to access and benefit from the offered services.

2.3.3 Floor-Ceiling Pricing

"Floor Price and Ceiling Price Model" is typically used in the pricing strategy of certain cloud service products. In this model, customers reach an agreement with the cloud service provider to ensure they will not pay more than a certain range of fees while using the service.

- **Floor Price:** This is the minimum price that the customer has to pay. Even if the customer uses very few services, they will still be billed according to the floor price.

- **Ceiling Price:** This is the maximum price that the customer needs to pay. Even if the customer uses a large amount of services, the cost will not exceed the ceiling price. Once the ceiling price is reached, additional service usage will no longer incur fees.

This model is often used in cases where flexible pricing strategies are required, such as long-term contracts or large enterprise customers who wish to limit fluctuations in costs to some extent. The floor price and ceiling price model provides customers with a predictable fee structure and offers cloud service providers a stable revenue stream.

The floor-ceiling model provides customers with the ability to forecast and control costs. Customers can determine the minimum and maximum cost ranges, ensuring they stay within budget. With service fees capped, customers can avoid unexpected cost increases. Even if service usage exceeds expectations, costs will not surpass the ceiling price.

Customers have a negotiating advantage when discussing pricing with cloud service providers. They can request appropriate floor and ceiling prices to meet their budget and requirements.

The floor-ceiling model can bring the following benefits to CSPs:

1. **Stable Revenue Stream**: The floor-ceiling model helps CSPs ensure a stable revenue stream, even if there are fluctuations in customer service usage. Since service fees are capped, CSPs can predict and plan revenue to some extent.

2. **Enhanced Customer Satisfaction**: By offering predictable cost structures, the floor-ceiling model can improve customer satisfaction. Customers can better control costs and avoid unexpected fee increases, thereby increasing trust and loyalty to the CSP.

3. **Competitive Advantage**: Adopting the floor-ceiling model can help CSPs stand out in a competitive market. Transparent, flexible, and predictable pricing strategies can attract more customers and increase market share.

4. **Customer Relationships**: The floor-ceiling model can strengthen the cooperation between CSPs and customers. By negotiating appropriate floor and ceiling prices with customers, CSPs can better meet their needs and establish long-term partnerships.

While bringing benefits, the floor-ceiling model also presents the following challenges to CSPs:

1. **Cost Management:** Managing costs can be challenging for CSPs under the floor-ceiling model. Despite capped revenue, unexpected increases in service usage may require CSPs to incur additional expenses, such as providing more resources or expanding infrastructure capacity.

2. **Pricing Strategy Complexity:** Setting appropriate floor and ceiling prices may require complex pricing strategy development and optimization. CSPs must balance customer needs, market competition, cost pressures, and revenue goals to determine the most competitive pricing scheme.

3. **Risk Exposure:** The floor-ceiling model may increase CSPs' risk exposure. While service usage is capped, if customer usage falls significantly below the floor price, CSPs may

face the risk of revenue decline and need to manage this risk effectively.

4. **Market Adaptability:** The floor-ceiling model may not be suitable for all types of cloud service products or customer segments. Some customers may prefer more flexible pricing models and may be reluctant to be subject to ceiling restrictions. Therefore, CSPs need to adjust pricing strategies based on market demand and customer feedback.

2.3.4 "Saving Plan" Pricing

A Saving Plan is a pricing model for cloud computing services that allows customers to prepay a certain amount to obtain the right to use resources for a period of time in the future. This prepayment is typically associated with the usage of resources offered by the cloud service provider, and customers can receive a certain percentage of resource discounts based on their prepaid amount and term.

Saving Plans typically apply to specific types of resources or services, such as virtual machine instances, storage space, or data transfer, and usually have fixed plan durations, such as one year or three years. The goal of Saving Plans is to help customers optimize costs, reduce the overall cost of resource usage, and provide a certain degree of flexibility and budget control.

The detailed structure of a Saving Plan typically includes the following components:

1. **Resource Type:** Saving Plans are usually specific to certain types of resources offered by the cloud service provider. These resources can include virtual machine instances, storage capacity, data transfer, or other services.

2. **Commitment:** Customers commit to a certain amount of usage of the specified resource type over a defined period, typically one or three years. This commitment is usually expressed in terms of a dollar amount or usage quantity.

3. **Payment Options:** Customers have flexibility in how they pay for the Saving Plan. They can choose to pay upfront for the entire commitment period, which often offers the highest discount, or they can opt for a partial upfront payment combined with ongoing usage-based payments.

4. **Discount Rate:** Based on the commitment amount and payment option chosen, customers receive a discount rate on the specified resource usage. This discount rate is applied to the standard on-demand pricing for the resource type.

5. **Flexibility:** Saving Plans may offer flexibility in terms of resource usage within the commitment period. Customers may be able to adjust their usage levels within certain limits without affecting the overall commitment amount or discount rate.

6. **Applicability:** Saving Plans may apply to specific regions or availability zones within the cloud provider's infrastructure. Customers should ensure that the Saving Plan they purchase covers the regions or zones where they expect to use the specified resources.

For customers, Saving Plans offer significant cost savings compared to PAYG pricing, especially for customers with predictable usage patterns or long-term commitments. The discounts provided through Saving Plans can result in substantial cost reductions for cloud services.

At the same time, Saving Plans often provide flexibility in terms of payment options, allowing customers to choose between upfront payments or a combination of upfront and recurring payments. This flexibility enables customers to align their payment schedules with their cash flow needs.

But there is also a little bit challenge for customers, especially the understanding the terms, conditions, and pricing structures of Saving Plans can be complex, especially for customers with diverse or dynamic usage patterns. Customers may require careful analysis and planning to determine the most cost-effective Saving Plan options for their needs.

2.4 Product Presentation

The product presentation of a cloud product refers to how the product is visually and interactively showcased to potential customers. It encompasses various elements to effectively communicate the product's features, functionality, pricing, and value proposition in a compelling and engaging manner.

Typically, cloud service providers showcase all their products on their official website. These product pages usually include the following:

1. **Product Overview:** A brief introduction to the product, including its main features, advantages, and use cases.

2. **Features and Capabilities:** Detailed listing of the product's features and capabilities, allowing customers to understand the services it can provide.

3. **Pricing Information:** Display of the product's pricing plans and fee structures, including differences in features and prices for different packages.

4. **Technical Support:** Provision of technical support information related to the product, including contact details, service level agreements (SLAs), and frequently asked questions (FAQs).

5. **Customer Case Studies:** Showcasing customer cases and success stories to demonstrate the product's value and effectiveness in real-world applications.

6. **Latest Updates:** Providing the latest information about product updates, new feature releases, and industry trends to keep customers informed.

7. **Purchase Entry:** Offering ways to contact the sales team for more information or to inquire about purchasing the product or providing an entry to be ordered online.

Through this information, customers can gain a comprehensive understanding of the products offered by the cloud service provider and make choices that best fit their needs.

The term "product presentation" not only refers to the product showcase on the official website to customers and potential clients but also encompasses product display to the sales team, sales partners, and other teams involved in product sales and service procedure within and outside the CSPs.

A good example of a well-crafted product presentation for cloud products is the AWS (Amazon Web Services) product catalog in website. AWS provides a comprehensive and user-friendly catalog that effectively conveys the features, benefits, and pricing of its various cloud services.

The AWS product catalog is organized in a structured manner, making it easy for customers to browse and explore different services. Each service is accompanied by detailed descriptions, use cases, pricing information, and technical specifications. Additionally, AWS offers interactive demos, tutorials, case studies, and customer testimonials to further illustrate the value proposition of its cloud services.

AWS product catalog serves as a valuable resource for customers to understand the wide range of cloud solutions available and make informed decisions based on their specific needs and requirements.

This section provides detailed explanations of key parts in product presentation.

2.4.1 Functional Features

Functional features can be difficult to understand for cloud and AI products due to their complexity and technical nature. Unlike tangible products with physical attributes, cloud and AI products often involve abstract concepts and advanced technologies that may not be familiar to all users.

Additionally, the rapid pace of innovation in these fields means that new features and capabilities are constantly being introduced, further complicating the understanding of product functionality.

Furthermore, the terminology used in cloud and AI can be highly technical and may require specialized knowledge to fully comprehend. As a result, users may struggle to grasp the full range of functional features offered by these products, making effective communication and education essential for ensuring their successful adoption and utilization.

Let's take Image Recognition as an example, the function specification can be breakdown into:

- *Object Detection: The ability to identify and locate objects within images, including their class labels and bounding boxes.*

- *Image Classification: Categorizing images into predefined classes or categories based on their visual content, such as identifying animals, vehicles, or landmarks.*

- *Facial Recognition: Recognizing and identifying human faces within images, often used for authentication, surveillance, or personalization purposes.*

- *Scene Recognition: Classifying entire scenes or environments depicted in images, such as indoor vs. outdoor scenes, landscapes, or urban environments.*

- *Image Segmentation: Partitioning images into meaningful regions or segments, enabling more precise analysis and understanding of visual content.*

- *Feature Extraction: Extracting relevant features or descriptors from images, such as color histograms, texture patterns, or key points, to represent visual characteristics.*

- *Image Similarity Matching: Comparing images to find similarities or matches based on visual content, useful for content-based image retrieval or recommendation systems.*

- *Object Tracking: Following the movement or trajectory of objects across multiple frames or images in a sequence, often used in video surveillance or augmented reality applications.*

How to make customers understand and accept so many functional specifications and be willing to pay for them. This requires service providers to put effort into the design of functional expression.

Presenting the functional features of a cloud product to customers requires a strategic approach to effectively communicate its value proposition and capabilities.

Providers must identify the key functional features of cloud product that align with customer needs and deliver the most value. Prioritize these features based on their importance and relevance to your target audience.

Simplify language and graphics: Use clear and concise language and graphics to describe the product's functionality, avoiding overly technical or difficult-to-understand terminology and concepts.

The most important aspect is to link the product's functional specifications with customer value. Customers need to understand the value each different functional specification brings and the differences between them.

2.4.2 Pricing Introduction

Due to the complexity of its functional features and the vast number of specifications, pricing information for cloud products can often be quite intricate. Therefore, when presenting pricing information to customers, special attention should be paid to the following points:

- **Clarity and Simplicity:** Present pricing information in a concise and clear manner, avoiding excessive use of technical terms or jargon to ensure customers can easily understand.

- **Transparency:** Ensure pricing information is transparent and easy to understand. Avoid hidden fees or unclear pricing structures that may confuse customers. Provide a breakdown of costs and charges to promote transparency.

- **Value Communication:** Clearly communicate the product's value proposition and advantages, emphasizing the relationship between the product's value and pricing. Explain to customers the product's value proposition and pricing strategy, helping them understand the true value and return on investment of the product.

- **Method to Inquiry:** Convenient browsing and querying methods, in addition to page-based queries, often require the ability to provide structured pricing information to customers via API.

Pricing based on SKU can effectively meet the specific requirements of cloud products in terms of simplicity, transparency, value communication, and query efficiency.

Using SKU (Stock Keeping Unit) to price the functional features of cloud products offers several benefits:

1. **Precision:** SKU-based pricing allows for precise pricing of individual functional features, ensuring that customers only pay for the specific features they need.

2. **Transparency:** By breaking down the pricing into individual SKUs for each functional feature, customers can see exactly what they are paying for, enhancing transparency and trust.

3. **Customization:** SKU-based pricing enables customization of quotes based on the unique requirements of each customer. Customers can select the specific combination of features they need, resulting in personalized pricing.

4. **Ease of Comparison:** With SKU-based pricing, customers can easily compare the prices of different features across products, facilitating informed decision-making.

5. **Scalability:** SKUs can be easily scaled and adjusted as the product evolves or new features are added. This flexibility ensures that pricing remains accurate and relevant over time.

6. **Efficiency:** Using SKUs streamlines the pricing process for both customers and sales teams, reducing the time and effort required to generate quotes and process orders.

Overall, SKU-based pricing enhances precision, transparency, customization, and efficiency in pricing cloud products, leading to improved customer satisfaction and sales effectiveness.

Here's an example of pricing based on SKU for an AI product:

AI Model Hosting Service

SKU	Description	Price (per month)
AI-001	Basic AI Model Hosting (1 model, 1000 API calls/day)	$50
AI-002	Standard AI Model Hosting (5 models, 5000 API calls/day)	$150
AI-003	Advanced AI Model Hosting (Unlimited models, 10000 API calls/day)	$300

In this example, different SKUs represent different tiers of AI model hosting services offered by the provider, each with its own price per month. Customers can select the SKU that aligns with their usage needs and budget constraints.

2.4.3 Interactive Demo

Interactive demos play a crucial role in showcasing the capabilities and benefits of cloud and AI products for several reasons.

Firstly, Interactive demos engage potential customers more effectively than static content like text or images. They allow users to actively explore the product's features and functionalities, leading to better understanding and retention of information.

Secondly, Interactive demos provide users with a hands-on experience of the product, allowing them to interact with its interface and test its functionalities in a simulated environment. This can help build trust and confidence in the product's capabilities.

After that, cloud and AI industry, complex concepts, such as machine learning algorithms or cloud infrastructure, can be difficult to grasp through text or static visuals alone. Interactive demos use visualizations, animations, and simulations to help users visualize abstract concepts more easily.

Lastly, Interactive demos can help users make informed decisions about whether the product meets their requirements and expectations. By allowing users to interact with the product in a risk-free environment, demos can help alleviate concerns and address objections before making a purchase decision.

For an AI product, an interactive demo might involve a sandbox environment where users can experiment with different machine learning models. They could upload datasets, train models, and visualize the results in real-time. The demo could also include interactive tutorials to guide users through the process of building and evaluating AI models.

2.4.4 Case Study

Case studies provide tangible examples of how cloud products have been successfully implemented in real-world scenarios. They showcase the practical application of the product, helping potential customers understand its functionality and benefits in context.

By showcasing successful implementations and positive outcomes, case studies help build trust and credibility with potential customers. They provide social proof that the product delivers on its promises and can effectively address the needs and challenges of similar businesses.

Case studies often highlight specific challenges or pain points that customers were facing before adopting the cloud product. This allows potential customers to see themselves in the story and understand how the product can help alleviate their own pain points or challenges.

Case studies often include metrics and data that demonstrate the return on investment (ROI) or the value delivered by the cloud product. This helps potential customers quantify the benefits they can expect to achieve by investing in the product, making the value proposition more compelling.

Overall, case studies play a vital role by providing compelling evidence of the value and effectiveness of cloud products, helping to overcome objections, build trust, and ultimately drive purchase decisions.

When creating a case study, it's important to avoid the following common mistakes:

1. **Lack of Customer Authorization and Consent**: Ensure explicit authorization and consent from the customer before publishing any case study. Unauthorized disclosure of customer information may violate privacy policies and damage trust with the customer.

2. **Ignoring Key Details of Customer Story**: Make sure the case study includes key details of the customer story, including the problem, solution, and outcome. These details

are crucial for showcasing the actual impact of the product and the customer's success.

3. **Exaggerating Product Effects**: Avoid exaggerating the product's features or effects. Honestly describe the product's advantages and limitations to establish a truthful and trustworthy case, as overstating may lead to customer disappointment and trust breakdown.

4. **Neglecting Quantitative Results**: Provide objective data and metrics to quantify the product's effects and value. These data can include specific numbers such as cost savings, efficiency improvements, revenue growth, etc., helping customers better understand the product's ROI.

5. **Being Overly Technical**: Avoid using overly specialized or technical terminology and language that non-technical readers may find difficult to understand. Ensure the content of the case study is concise, clear, and understandable to general readers.

6. **Lack of Customer Involvement and Feedback**: Collaborate closely with the customer when writing the case study, seeking their involvement and feedback. Customer involvement helps ensure the accuracy and authenticity of the case study, providing deeper insights and stories.

7. **Ignoring Customer Privacy and Confidentiality**: Respect customer privacy and confidentiality when publishing the case study. Avoid disclosing sensitive information or trade secrets, ensuring the case study complies with the customer's confidentiality requirements.

By avoiding these mistakes and focusing on creating genuine, objective, and quantified case studies, you can effectively showcase the product's value and impact, enhancing customer trust and recognition.

2.4.5 Product Catalogue

The product catalog is important for conveying the value of a product because it serves as a centralized repository of information about all available products and services offered by a company. It provides a comprehensive overview of the company's offerings, making it easier for customers to browse and compare different options.

A well-organized product catalog categorizes products into logical groupings or categories based on their type, functionality, or intended use. This makes it easier for customers and sales team to navigate the catalog and find products that meet their specific needs or preferences.

A product catalog can also be used as a tool for cross-selling and upselling related products or complementary services. By showcasing additional products that complement the customer's initial purchase or offering bundle deals, companies can increase the average order value and drive additional revenue.

Tsutaya Books in Japan is a typical example of creative product catalog arrangement. In this bookstore, product display is ingeniously designed to showcase various usage scenarios. Apart from books, Tsutaya Books also offers a variety of media and entertainment products such as music, movies, and games. The bookstore is arranged like a small cultural and entertainment hub, not only selling books but also creating a pleasant environment for reading and relaxation. This creative product arrangement has attracted many customers, making Tsutaya Books a popular cultural gathering place.

The importance of product catalog extends beyond conveying the functional features of the product; it also lies in communicating the product's value to customers and establishing resonance with them.

By clearly showcasing the advantages and benefits of the product, the product catalog can help customers better understand its true value and stimulate their desire to purchase. Therefore, a well-designed product catalog not only attracts customer attention but also facilitates sales and fosters brand loyalty.

2.4.6 Product Portfolio

A robust product portfolio allows cloud providers to offer a diverse range of services to meet the varying needs of different customers. By offering a comprehensive set of services, providers can attract a wider customer base and cater to different industries, use cases, and geographical regions.

Especially in cloud industry, providing multiple cloud products that complement each other to form a complete solution is highly attractive to customers. Customers can obtain various cloud products they need from a single provider without dealing with multiple vendors. This simplifies the procurement process, saving time and effort.

Different products from the same provider typically integrate and work together more effectively, avoiding compatibility issues between different products. This ensures the stability and reliability of the entire system.

Providers can tailor solutions to meet customers' specific needs and business scenarios, including combinations, configurations, and pricing models of different products, thus better satisfying customers' personalized requirements.

Additionally, combining multiple cloud products can generate synergistic effects, enhancing overall performance and efficiency. For example, combining CDN and WAF products can accelerate content delivery while protecting website security, improving user experience.

For cloud providers, enriching their product portfolio and creating the synergistic effects mentioned above doesn't necessarily require developing all these products in-house. Apart from their core products, cloud providers can collaborate with third-party product vendors in various forms, such as OEM, ODM, OBM, and others. These collaborations help in enriching the product portfolio.

How to efficiently collaborate with third-party vendors will be elaborately discussed in the "Partner" chapter of this book.

2.5 GTM Strategy

GTM stands for "Go-To-Market" strategy. It refers to the plan of action that outlines how a company will bring its products or services to market, attract customers, and achieve competitive advantage.

A GTM strategy encompasses various elements, including product positioning, target market identification, marketing channels, sales tactics, pricing strategies, and distribution methods.

The goal of a GTM strategy is to effectively launch and promote products or services, capture demand, acquire customers, and drive revenue growth. It involves aligning the organization's resources, capabilities, and messaging to address customer needs and market opportunities. A well-defined GTM strategy is essential for successful product launches, market penetration, and sustainable business growth.

2.5.1 Positioning & Proposition

Product positioning refers to the perception of a product in the minds of consumers relative to competing products.

It involves creating a distinct image and identity for a product in the marketplace that differentiates it from others and appeals to the target audience. This positioning is typically based on various factors such as the product's features, benefits, price, quality, and the needs and preferences of the target market. Effective product positioning helps companies attract and retain customers by communicating the unique value proposition of their product and establishing a competitive advantage.

Please note that there is another similar concept called "Product Value Proposition".

The product value proposition is a statement that communicates the unique benefits and value that a product or service offers to customers. It answers the question, "Why should customers choose this product over others?" The value proposition highlights the specific problems or needs the product addresses, the benefits it delivers, and why it's better than alternative solutions. It's essentially the promise of value that the product provides to customers.

While product positioning focuses on how a product is perceived relative to competitors, the value proposition focuses on articulating the unique benefits and value that the product offers to customers. However, effective product positioning often involves communicating the product's value proposition in a way that resonates with the target audience. Therefore, they are closely related concepts that work together to create a compelling offering in the market.

Cloud and AI markets are highly competitive, with numerous vendors offering similar solutions. Effective product positioning helps differentiate your offerings from competitors by highlighting unique features, benefits, or use cases. Clear positioning ensures that your product resonates with the right audience and addresses their specific needs and pain points.

Product positioning provides a framework for marketing and sales teams to align their strategies and messaging. It ensures consistency in how your offerings are presented and promoted across different channels.

Creating product positioning for cloud and AI products involves several steps to ensure clarity, relevance, and differentiation in the market. Here's a systematic approach:

1. **Understand Your Target Audience**: Begin by conducting thorough market research to understand your target audience's needs, pain points, preferences, and buying behaviors. Identify the industries, businesses, or personas that are most likely to benefit from your cloud and AI products.

2. **Define Unique Selling Points (USPs)**: Identify the key features, functionalities, or capabilities that set your cloud and AI products apart from competitors. These could include advanced algorithms, scalability, flexibility, ease of integration, security measures, or industry-specific solutions.

3. **Craft a Value Proposition**: Develop a compelling value proposition that clearly articulates the benefits and outcomes your cloud and AI products offer to customers. Focus on how your offerings address specific challenges, improve efficiency, drive innovation, reduce costs, or generate measurable results.

4. **Identify Market Positioning**: Determine where your cloud and AI products fit within the market landscape. Assess competitors' offerings and positioning to identify gaps or opportunities for differentiation. Decide whether your products will be positioned as premium, affordable, niche-focused, industry-specific, or innovation-driven solutions.

5. **Create Positioning Statements**: Develop concise positioning statements that succinctly communicate the unique value proposition of your cloud and AI products.

These statements should address the target audience, key benefits, competitive differentiation, and overall positioning in the market.

6. **Tailor Messaging for Segments**: Customize your product positioning and messaging for different market segments, industries, or buyer personas. Highlight specific use cases, benefits, and value propositions that resonate with each audience segment's unique needs and priorities.

7. **Validate with Stakeholders**: Socialize your product positioning with internal stakeholders, including product managers, marketers, sales teams, and executives. Gather feedback and insights to ensure alignment with overall business objectives, market realities, and customer expectations.

8. **Test and Iterate**: Conduct market testing and validation to assess the effectiveness of your product positioning with target customers. Use surveys, focus groups, interviews, and A/B testing to gather feedback and refine your messaging as needed.

9. **Integrate Across Channels**: Ensure consistency in your product positioning across all marketing and sales channels, including website content, sales collateral, advertising campaigns, social media, email communications, and customer support interactions.

10. **Monitor and Adapt**: Continuously monitor market dynamics, customer feedback, and competitive developments to stay agile and responsive. Be prepared to adjust your product positioning strategy as needed to maintain relevance and effectiveness in the evolving cloud and AI landscape.

By following these steps, you can develop a compelling and differentiated product positioning strategy for your cloud and AI products that resonates with target customers and drives business growth.

2.5.2 Seed Customer

A "seed customer" refers to the initial set of customers that a company targets when introducing a new product or service. These customers are typically early adopters or influential individuals who are willing to try out the product or service in its early stages. Seed customers play a crucial role in providing feedback, spreading word-of-mouth referrals, and validating the product or service before it is launched to a wider audience. They serve as the foundation for the product's growth and success.

Seed customers provide valuable feedback on the product's features, functionality, and user experience. This feedback helps the company identify areas for improvement and make necessary adjustments before launching to a wider audience.

Seed customers validate the product's value proposition and market fit. Their willingness to use the product demonstrates initial interest and helps build credibility for the offering. Working closely with seed customers allows the company to iterate on the product based on real-world usage and feedback. This iterative development process leads to a more refined and polished product upon wider release.

Furthermore, satisfied seed customers can become advocates for the product, sharing their positive experiences with others in their network. This word-of-mouth marketing can help generate buzz and attract additional customers.

Finding seed customers for cloud and AI products involves targeted outreach and strategic networking. Here are some steps to help you identify and engage potential seed customers:

1. **Events Attending**: Attend industry conferences, trade shows, and networking events where you are likely to meet individuals and companies interested in innovative technologies. Engage in conversations, exchange contact information, and follow up with potential leads.

2. **Online Communities**: Join relevant online communities, forums, and social media groups where professionals in your target market gather. Participate in discussions, share insights about your product, and connect with individuals who show interest in your offering.

3. **Referrals**: Leverage your existing network and ask for referrals from colleagues, partners, and mentors. They may be able to introduce you to potential seed customers who could benefit from your cloud and AI product.

4. **Cold Outreach**: Reach out directly to individuals or companies that align with your target market and could serve as potential seed customers. Craft personalized messages highlighting the value proposition of your product and offering them an opportunity to be early adopters.

5. **Pilot Programs**: Offer free or discounted trials of your product to selected prospects in exchange for their feedback and participation in a pilot program. This allows you to test your product with real users and gather valuable insights for improvement.

6. **Industry Influencers**: Identify industry influencers, thought leaders, and experts who can help amplify your

message and connect you with potential seed customers. Build relationships with these individuals and explore opportunities for collaboration or endorsement.

7. **Partnerships**: Seek out strategic partnerships with complementary businesses or service providers that already have access to your target market. Collaborating with these partners can help you reach potential seed customers more effectively.

By implementing these strategies and approaches, you can identify and engage seed customers who are willing to test and provide feedback on your cloud and AI products, laying the foundation for broader market adoption.

2.5.3 Distribution Channel

Distribution channels are crucial for product Go-To-Market (GTM) strategies because they serve as the means through which products reach customers.

Distribution channels enable companies to reach a broader audience by leveraging existing networks and partnerships. They provide access to different market segments, regions, and customer demographics, allowing companies to expand their reach beyond their immediate geographical area.

Utilizing distribution channels can be cost-effective compared to building and managing direct sales channels. By partnering with distributors, wholesalers, or retailers, companies can avoid the overhead costs associated with maintaining in-house sales and distribution teams, logistics, and infrastructure.

Distribution partners often possess specialized knowledge, experience, and resources that can enhance the success of product launches and sales efforts. They may offer valuable insights into local market dynamics, customer preferences, and competitive landscape, as well as provide marketing, sales, and technical support to drive product adoption.

Distribution channels enable companies to scale their operations and reach larger customer bases without significant investments in infrastructure or personnel. By tapping into established distribution networks, companies can quickly scale up their sales and distribution efforts to meet growing demand and expand into new markets.

Diversifying distribution channels helps mitigate risks associated with dependence on single sales channels or markets. By spreading sales across multiple channels and geographic regions, companies can reduce their exposure to market fluctuations, regulatory changes, or disruptions in specific industries or regions.

For cloud and AI products, several distribution channels can be suitable, depending on factors such as target market, product complexity, customer preferences, and competitive landscape. Here are some distribution channels commonly used for cloud and AI products:

1. **Online Marketplaces**: Leveraging online platforms such as Amazon Web Services (AWS) Marketplace, Microsoft Azure Marketplace, or Google Cloud Marketplace allows cloud and AI product vendors to reach a wide audience of potential customers who are already engaged in cloud computing and AI-related activities. These marketplaces provide a convenient platform for customers to discover, evaluate, and purchase software solutions, including cloud services, AI algorithms, and machine learning models.

2. **Direct Sales**: Direct sales channels involve selling products directly to customers through in-house sales teams or

dedicated sales representatives. This approach is particularly suitable for high-value, complex cloud and AI solutions that require customized solutions, extensive consultation, and ongoing support. Direct sales enable vendors to establish direct relationships with customers, understand their unique needs, and tailor solutions to meet specific requirements.

3. **Partner Reseller Networks**: Partnering with value-added resellers (VARs), system integrators (SIs), consultants, and managed service providers (MSPs) allows cloud and AI product vendors to extend their reach and tap into established distribution networks. VARs and SIs can bundle cloud and AI products with complementary services, such as implementation, customization, training, and support, offering customers a comprehensive solution and helping vendors penetrate new markets and verticals.

4. **OEM and White-Label Partnerships**: Original equipment manufacturer (OEM) and white-label partnerships involve licensing or rebranding cloud and AI products for resale by other companies under their own brand names. This approach enables vendors to reach new customer segments, expand their product offerings, and capitalize on the distribution channels and customer relationships of partner organizations. OEM and white-label partnerships are common in industries such as telecommunications, healthcare, and finance, where companies seek to integrate cloud and AI capabilities into their existing product portfolios.

5. **Online Direct Sales and E-commerce Platforms**: Establishing an online presence through company websites, e-commerce platforms, and digital marketing channels allows cloud and AI product vendors to engage with customers directly and facilitate self-service purchasing experiences. By optimizing their online storefronts, leveraging search

engine optimization (SEO), and employing digital marketing strategies such as content marketing, social media, and email campaigns, vendors can attract, educate, and convert prospects into customers in a cost-effective manner.

6. **Developer Communities and Marketplaces**: Targeting developer communities and marketplaces, such as GitHub, Docker Hub, or Kaggle, can be an effective way to promote cloud and AI products among technical audiences, including software developers, data scientists, and machine learning engineers. By providing software development kits (SDKs), APIs, sample code, tutorials, and community forums, vendors can encourage experimentation, innovation, and collaboration around their products, driving adoption and generating developer mindshare.

Ultimately, the most suitable distribution channels for cloud and AI products will depend on factors such as product complexity, target market characteristics, competitive dynamics, and business objectives. A diversified approach that combines multiple distribution channels can help vendors maximize their market coverage, customer reach, and revenue opportunities while adapting to evolving market conditions and customer preferences.

2.6 Product Performance

In this book, "product performance" primarily refers to how well a product meets business and customer experience expectations rather than purely technical metrics. This could include aspects such as the product's ability to deliver value to customers, meet their needs effectively, and provide a positive user experience. It may also encompass factors like reliability, ease of use, functionality, and overall satisfaction with the product.

Product performance management becomes crucial for ensuring that the product aligns with business goals and meets customer needs effectively.

Continuous Product Performance monitoring generates valuable data insights that can inform product development, optimization, and strategic decision-making. By analyzing performance metrics, product teams can identify areas for improvement and prioritize initiatives that enhance the overall product experience.

2.6.1 Product Experience

Product experience plays a significant role in determining the success of a product, including cloud and AI products. A positive product experience leads to higher user satisfaction. When users find a product easy to use, intuitive, and effective in meeting their needs, they are more likely to continue using it and recommend it to others.

A compelling product experience encourages users to engage more frequently and deeply with the product. Engaged users are more likely to explore different features, provide feedback, and become loyal advocates for the product.

A differentiated product experience sets a product apart from competitors in the market. By delivering unique value propositions, innovative features, and superior usability, a product can gain a competitive edge and attract more customers.

A positive product experience reduces barriers to adoption and accelerates the customer acquisition process. When potential customers have positive interactions with a product, they are more likely to convert into paying customers and generate revenue for the business.

In summary, product experience directly influences user satisfaction, engagement, retention, loyalty, competitive advantage, brand reputation, word-of-mouth marketing, customer acquisition, and product iteration. By prioritizing and optimizing the product experience, businesses can drive product success and achieve their strategic objectives.

However, Cloud products present challenges in delivering a good product experience due to several reasons:

- **User Onboarding:** Cloud products may require users to undergo complex onboarding processes, including account setup, configuration, and training. Simplifying the onboarding experience while providing comprehensive guidance and support can enhance the product experience but requires careful design and execution.

- **Complexity:** Cloud products often offer a wide range of features and capabilities, making them inherently complex. Managing this complexity while ensuring ease of use and intuitive navigation can be challenging for product designers and developers.

- **User Interface Design:** Designing an intuitive and user-friendly interface for cloud products can be challenging, especially when dealing with complex workflows and large datasets. Balancing functionality with simplicity and ensuring consistency across different screens and devices is crucial for a good product experience.

- **Feedback Loop:** Maintaining a feedback loop with users to gather insights, address issues, and incorporate user feedback into product improvements is essential for enhancing the product experience. However, managing this feedback loop effectively can be challenging, particularly for widely distributed cloud products with diverse user bases.

Product experience encompasses various aspects such as usability, functionality, emotional appeal, and the overall value delivered to the user. While it is subjective and can vary from person to person, there are several objective measures and methodologies that can be used to assess and evaluate product experience:

1. **Usability Testing:** Conducting usability tests to observe how easily and efficiently users can accomplish tasks with the product. This involves tasks like navigation, data entry, and completing specific actions within the product.

2. **User Surveys and Feedback:** Collecting feedback from users through surveys, interviews, or feedback forms to understand their satisfaction levels, pain points, and areas for improvement.

3. **User Analytics:** Analyzing user behavior and interactions within the product using tools like heatmaps, click tracking, and session recordings to identify patterns, trends, and areas of friction.

4. **Net Promoter Score (NPS):** Measuring customer loyalty and satisfaction by asking users how likely they are to recommend the product to others. This provides a quantitative measure of overall satisfaction and brand advocacy.

5. **Customer Support Metrics:** Monitoring metrics related to customer support interactions such as response time, resolution time, and customer satisfaction scores to gauge the quality of support provided and its impact on the overall product experience.

6. **User Retention and Churn Rates:** Tracking user retention rates and churn rates over time to understand how satisfied users are with the product and whether they continue to use it or switch to alternatives.

7. **Competitive Analysis:** Benchmarking the product experience against competitors and industry standards to identify areas of strength and weakness and inform product improvement efforts.

By leveraging these objective measures and methodologies, organizations can gain valuable insights into the product experience and identify opportunities to enhance usability, functionality, and overall user satisfaction.

2.6.2 Product Cost

The cost of a product is crucial for its commercial success because high costs may reduce profits or even lead to losses. While a product may have powerful features, if the cost is too high, customers may be unwilling to pay that price, affecting the product's market acceptance and sales volume. Therefore, in product design, cost factors must be considered, and efforts should be made to reduce costs to ensure the product has a competitive price and achieves sustainable commercial success in the market.

This is why the cost of the product is included as part of the product performance for explanation and description.

However, calculating the costs of cloud and AI products is a rather complex task.

The biggest characteristic of cloud products is the use of virtualization technology to achieve resource sharing across the entire network. Users no longer perceive the physical aspects of servers, networking, and storage; instead, they utilize these technological capabilities logically. Additionally, with the development of cloud-native technologies, the cost calculation for upper-layer products provided based on underlying cloud products becomes even more complex.

Cost accounting for products is a professional financial activity. Typically, it involves considering the following costs:

1. **Research and Development (R&D) Costs**: The manpower, time, and resources invested in developing new products or services.

2. **Material Costs**: The cost of raw materials, components, and other materials required for product production.

3. **Marketing Costs**: Expenses incurred in promoting and marketing products or services, including advertising, promotions, and marketing expenses.

4. **Sales Costs**: Expenses related to selling products or services, such as sales team salaries and commissions, and sales channel expenses.

5. **Delivery Costs**: Costs associated with delivering products or services to customers, including logistics, transportation, and installation costs.

6. **Service Costs**: Expenses incurred in providing after-sales service and support to customers, including customer service staff salaries and repair costs.

7. **Administrative Costs**: General expenses associated with managing and operating the business, such as office space rent and administrative staff salaries.

For companies with multiple product lines or product types, it is necessary to allocate the above costs to different products in a reasonable manner to reflect the profit and loss situation of individual products. This helps companies evaluate the profitability of products, optimize cost structures, and formulate appropriate pricing strategies and business decisions.

For cloud products, it's important to consider the cost curve alongside increasing user volume and innovative pricing models.

For example, with different pricing models such as spot instances and reserved instances, the cost composition and calculation can vary significantly for virtual machine products.

2.6.3 Product Profit

Profit calculation for cloud products poses a challenge for the finance departments of cloud providers due to several reasons:

1. **Complex Cost Structure**: Cloud products often have intricate cost structures involving various components such as infrastructure, maintenance, support, and overhead costs. Allocating these costs accurately across different products and services can be challenging.

2. **Data Complexity and Volume**: Profit calculation for cloud products relies on extensive data, including usage data, cost data, billing data, and customer data. Managing and analyzing large volumes of data from multiple sources can be challenging and may require advanced data analytics tools and techniques.

Macro-level product profit analysis and micro-level product profit analysis are two different methods used to analyze and evaluate the profitability of specific products.

Macro-level product profit analysis

Macro-level product profit analysis considers the profitability of a specific product or product line from an overall perspective, typically involving its contribution to the overall profits of the enterprise.

It focuses on analyzing the overall profit capability and contribution of a specific product, including total revenue, total costs, total profit, and other indicators.

Macro-level product profit analysis helps enterprise managers understand the contribution of a specific product to the overall profitability of the enterprise, enabling them to formulate overall product strategies and business decisions.

Micro-level product profit analysis

Micro-level product profit analysis considers the profitability of a specific product from a more detailed perspective, typically involving individual sales transactions or production processes.

It focuses on analyzing the profit capability and cost structure of individual sales orders or production batches of a specific product, including revenue, costs, profits, and other indicators for each transaction or batch.

Micro-level product profit analysis helps enterprise managers understand the profitability of a specific product in more detail, identifying profit bottlenecks and optimization opportunities to improve the profitability of the product.

In summary, both macro-level product profit analysis and micro-level product profit analysis are important management tools, each with its own applicable scenarios and advantages. Enterprises need to comprehensively apply these two methods based on specific circumstances to fully understand and manage the profitability of specific products.

2.6.4 Product Problem

Product problem analysis for cloud products involves identifying and addressing issues or challenges related to the functionality, performance, usability, reliability, and security of cloud-based services.

Product problem analysis is crucial for cloud and AI product.

Identifying and addressing product problems improves customer satisfaction by resolving issues that impact user experience, performance, and functionality. Satisfied customers are more likely to continue using the product and recommend it to others.

Analyzing product problems provides valuable insights into areas for improvement. By understanding common pain points and user challenges, product teams can prioritize enhancements and new features that address customer needs and preferences.

Product problem analysis can uncover opportunities for innovation and differentiation. By identifying unmet customer needs or pain points, product teams can develop innovative solutions that set their product apart from competitors and drive market leadership.

Ensuring accurate and efficient communication of product problems from the customer service department to the research and development (R&D) department is crucial for cloud computing service providers. This determines the ability of products to iterate and improve quickly. Here are some key steps and methods to achieve this goal:

1. **Establish Effective Communication Channels**: Ensure that effective communication channels are established

between the customer service and R&D departments. This can be achieved through regular meetings, communication platforms, emails, etc., to facilitate information exchange and sharing.

2. **Clarify Responsibilities and Processes**: Define the responsible individuals and processes for the transfer of product issues, ensuring clarity at each stage. Establish standardized issue reporting and tracking processes, including descriptions, priorities, and status tracking, to ensure accurate recording and monitoring of issues.

3. **Utilize Tools and System Support**: Use specialized issue tracking systems or customer relationship management (CRM) software to help the customer service department record and track product issues and seamlessly interface with the R&D department. These systems can provide features such as issue reporting, priority setting, automatic assignment, and status updates, enhancing the efficiency and accuracy of issue resolution.

4. **Foster a Culture of Collaboration**: Promote close cooperation and a culture of collaboration between the customer service and R&D departments. Hold regular cross-departmental meetings or communications to share product issues and solutions, discuss methods and strategies for product improvement together.

5. **Provide Timely Feedback and Updates**: The customer service department should promptly provide feedback to the R&D department on customer product issues and feedback, including specific descriptions, impact scope, and urgency. The R&D department should respond promptly and update issue statuses to ensure timely feedback and solutions for customers and the customer service department.

6. **Continuous Improvement and Optimization**: Regularly evaluate and optimize the issue transfer and resolution processes. Adjust and improve communication channels, tools, systems, and collaboration methods based on actual situations to enhance the efficiency and accuracy of product issue handling.

By implementing these methods and steps, cloud computing service providers can achieve accurate and efficient communication of product issues from the customer service department to the R&D department, thereby promoting rapid iteration and improvement of products, enhancing customer satisfaction, and product competitiveness.

2.7 Product Lifecycle

In the cloud service market, new products emerge constantly, leading to an increasing number of existing products. However, not every product can achieve comprehensive commercial success. Therefore, lifecycle management of all company products is crucial for improving operational efficiency, strategically positioning suitable products for their intended purposes, and concentrating resources to penetrate the market.

Positioning cloud products at different stages of the product lifecycle requires considering the current stage of the product and formulating corresponding strategies.

Introduction Stage

The product is newly launched or in the initial phase of market entry, aiming to attract market attention and establish brand awareness.

Company should focus on product promotion, marketing, and advertising to attract early adopters and potential customers. Pricing may be set lower to encourage market acceptance.

Growth Stage

The product starts gaining market share, with sales and user base gradually increasing. Company should increase marketing efforts to expand the customer base. Invest more resources in product research and development to meet growing demands. Pricing can be moderately increased to enhance profitability.

Maturity Stage

Market competition is intense, and product growth slows down but maintains a stable market position.

Company should emphasize product differentiation and value propositions to maintain a competitive advantage. Focus on customer satisfaction and loyalty, enhance product quality, and service levels. Consider cost reduction and operational efficiency optimization.

Decline Stage

Market share for the product decreases, and sales and profits are affected, possibly facing the risk of elimination.

Company should evaluate the product's sustainability and future growth potential. Consider exiting product lines that lack competitive advantages and redirect resources to more promising products or emerging markets.

Product lifecycle management is a mature topic, with numerous methods and tools available. This book will not delve into further detail on this matter.

This section focuses on the unique aspects of product lifecycle management in cloud and AI products.

2.7.1 Fail Fast

In the process of product management, it's crucial to maintain an objective attitude: not every product launched by a company will achieve success. It's essential to objectively assess products that are not performing well in the market and make timely decisions, such as withdrawing from the market or pivoting. Avoiding failure should not be the primary concern; instead, facing failure courageously is necessary. Even in the case of a failed product, valuable market and customer insights can be gained, deepening the company's understanding of specific domains, and laying the groundwork for the success of future products.

"Fail fast" is a skill that requires companies to have a comprehensive understanding of various metrics and make firm judgments on various situations during the product management process. Only then can they "fail fast" rather than linger on and become zombie products that drag down the company.

Here are examples of products that were once highly anticipated but ultimately failed to achieve commercial success due to various reasons, but company didn't define it as failure in time, leading to company struggles or bankruptcy:

1. Google Glass: This was a smart glasses product initially met with high expectations. However, due to issues related to privacy, security, and practicality, as well as limited public acceptance, the product did not achieve commercial success and was ultimately discontinued.
2. BlackBerry: This was once a popular smartphone product, but it gradually lost market share with the rise of Apple and Android systems. The company failed to adjust its strategy to adapt to market changes in time, leading to the decline of its smartphone business and eventual acquisition by other companies.

Failing fast in product management involves embracing a mindset of experimentation, learning, and quick adaptation. Here's how to implement it effectively:

1. **Set Clear Goals and Metrics:** Define specific, measurable goals and key performance indicators (KPIs) for your product. These metrics should align with your overall business objectives and help you track progress accurately.

2. **Experimentation Culture:** Foster a culture where experimentation and risk-taking are encouraged. Encourage team members to propose and test new ideas, features, and strategies. Create a safe environment where failure is seen as an opportunity for learning and improvement.

3. **Rapid Prototyping:** Develop prototypes or minimum viable products (MVPs) quickly to validate assumptions and gather feedback from users. Use agile methodologies to iterate rapidly based on user input and market insights.

4. **Continuous Testing and Feedback:** Implement continuous testing processes to gather data and feedback throughout the product development lifecycle. Conduct user testing, usability studies, and A/B testing to identify potential issues and opportunities for improvement early on.

5. **Iterative Development:** Break down product development into small, iterative cycles or sprints. Set short-term goals and milestones to track progress and adjust as needed. Focus on delivering incremental value to users with each iteration.

6. **Fail-Forward Mentality:** Embrace failures as learning opportunities and encourage team members to share their experiences openly. Analyze failures objectively to understand

what went wrong and why. Use these insights to pivot, iterate, or course-correct quickly.

7. **Data-Driven Decision Making:** Base decisions on data and evidence rather than assumptions or intuition. Use analytics tools to gather quantitative data on user behavior, engagement, and performance metrics. Use qualitative research methods to gain deeper insights into user needs and preferences.

8. **Leadership Support:** Ensure that senior leadership supports and reinforces the fail-fast approach. Communicate the importance of experimentation and learning as part of the organization's culture and values.

By embracing a fail-fast approach, product managers can identify and address issues early, minimize wasted resources, and ultimately increase the likelihood of success in delivering valuable products to market.

2.7.2 BCG Matrix

The Boston Consulting Group Matrix, abbreviated as the BCG Matrix, is an analytical tool proposed by the Boston Consulting Group for product portfolio management and strategic planning. This matrix evaluates products based on two dimensions: market share and market growth rate, dividing them into four quadrants: Stars, Question Marks, Cash Cows, and Dogs, to guide decision-making in product development and management.

1. **Stars:** Stars are products with high market share in high-growth markets, often requiring significant investment to sustain their growth. They have high market share and high market growth rate, necessitating continuous investment to

maintain competitive advantage and achieve long-term profit growth.

2. **Question Marks:** Question Marks are products with low market share in high-growth markets. These products typically require substantial investment and effort to increase their market share and potentially transition into Stars. Managers need to carefully assess the potential of Question Marks and decide whether to increase investment to accelerate their development or reduce investment to avoid losses.

3. **Cash Cows:** Cash Cows are products with high market share in low-growth markets. These products usually do not require significant investment but generate stable cash flow and profits. Managers often view Cash Cows as a stable source of income to support the development and growth of other products.

4. **Dogs:** Dogs are products with low market share in low-growth markets. These products often cannot generate substantial revenue for the company and may require continuous investment and support. Managers need to carefully assess the value of Dogs and consider exiting or restructuring these products to release resources and minimize losses.

Incorporating the Boston Consulting Group (BCG) Matrix into product lifecycle management can help companies better understand and manage the position and potential of their product portfolio, enabling them to formulate more effective management strategies and decisions.

Here are some methods for applying the BCG Matrix in product lifecycle management:

1. **Product Positioning:** Allocate products to different quadrants of the BCG Matrix based on their stage in the product lifecycle. For example, products in the growth stage may belong to the Stars quadrant, while products in the decline stage may belong to the Dogs quadrant.

2. **Resource Allocation:** Adjust resource allocation for different products in the portfolio based on the classification results of the BCG Matrix. Increase resource investment for Stars and Question Marks to support their further development and growth. Maintain stable resource allocation for Cash Cows to preserve stable income. Consider reducing resource investment or exiting the market for Dogs.

3. **Strategic Planning:** Formulate product lifecycle management strategies and tactics based on the classification results of the BCG Matrix. Develop growth and expansion strategies for Stars and Question Marks to accelerate market penetration and increase market share. Implement stabilization and profit maximization strategies for Cash Cows to maintain stable income. Consider exit or restructuring strategies for Dogs to minimize losses and release resources.

4. **Market Monitoring:** Regularly monitor product performance in the market, changes in the competitive environment, and the position and trends of products in the BCG Matrix. Based on monitoring results, adjust product lifecycle management strategies and measures timely to adapt to market changes and product development needs.

Integrating the BCG Matrix with product lifecycle management can help companies better manage and optimize their product portfolios, achieving long-term business goals. By allocating resources reasonably, formulating effective strategies, and adjusting strategies timely, companies can better adapt to market changes and product development needs, enhancing product competitiveness and profitability.

2.7.3 Product Retirement

Cloud products often host customer data and business applications. Product exiting improperly may jeopardize data security and integrity. A careful exit strategy ensures data migration and handling processes safeguard against data loss or breaches.

Improper or unlawful exits can lead to legal disputes and litigation, posing unnecessary legal risks and losses. A prudent exit strategy helps avoid legal disputes and ensures contracts and legal obligations are properly addressed.

A well-planned exit strategy helps maintain good relations with customers and minimizes negative impacts.

Customer Communication: Before deciding to exit a product, it's essential to communicate thoroughly with existing customers, providing reasonable explanations and transition plans. Ensure customers understand and accept the reasons for product discontinuation and assist them in smoothly transitioning to other solutions.

Data Migration: Ensure customers can easily migrate their data and workloads to other platforms or services. Provide migration tools and support to ensure data security and integrity.

Contract Termination: Handle product-related contract termination matters, including contract terms and conditions, refund policies, service termination dates, etc. Negotiate with customers and devise reasonable solutions to minimize potential legal disputes.

Technical Support: Continue to provide necessary technical support and services during the product exit process, ensuring customers can smoothly complete migration and transition. Address any issues and challenges customers may encounter, maintaining good customer relationships.

Data Security: Ensure customers' data security remains uncompromised during the product exit process. Take necessary measures to protect customer data, including data encryption, secure deletion, etc.

2.7.4 Total Lifetime Value

The total lifetime value (TLV) of a product refers to the total value created by the product for a company throughout its entire lifecycle. This includes all stages from product design, development, production, sales, marketing, customer service, to product retirement. TLV considers the product's contributions, including direct sales revenue, repurchase rate, customer satisfaction, word-of-mouth impact, brand loyalty, among other factors. By understanding and maximizing the total lifetime value of a product, companies can devise more effective strategies to enhance customer satisfaction, increase revenue, reduce costs, and elevate brand value.

CPSs should measure and evaluate the value of products to the company from the perspective of the entire product lifecycle. In this assessment, value is not solely measured by revenue. These values may include:

- **Customer Acquisition**: Introducing a product may attract new customers, expand the customer base, and lay the foundation for future growth.

- **Market Penetration**: Through product promotion and marketing, companies can strengthen their position in target markets, increasing market share and influence.

- **Cash Flow Contribution**: The cash flow generated from product sales is an important indicator of product economic performance but not the sole source of value.

3

CUSTOMER

Customer is one of the core assets for CSP business operations, so efficient and accurate management of customer information is crucial. Comprehensive collection and management of customer information ensure that all departments within CSP can accurately understand the customer's organizational structure, demand forecast, purchase intentions, and problem complaints.

For CSPs, most of customers are various entities such as enterprises, governments, and research institutions. The term "customer" for CSPs is not just a simple entity; it comprises multiple departments, project teams, and various roles. Being able to collect and manage this dispersed customer information and integrate them with the transaction, usage, and payment processes of cloud products is crucial for both CSPs and customers.

This chapter will explore how to manage and utilize customer information in the industry of technology products such as cloud computing and AI.

3.1 Customer Acquisition

Customer acquisition refers to the process of attracting and converting potential customers into actual paying customers. It involves various marketing and sales strategies aimed at identifying, targeting, and persuading individuals or organizations to purchase products or services offered by a business. Customer acquisition efforts typically include activities such as advertising, content marketing, search engine optimization (SEO), social media marketing, email marketing, and sales outreach. The goal of customer acquisition is to grow the customer base and increase revenue for the business.

Customer acquisition for cloud products often involves some unique considerations compared to traditional products or services.

Products in the cloud computing industry are specialized technical products and are not as widely needed by ordinary users as consumer goods. Moreover, different types of cloud products serve vastly different types of enterprises. Therefore, it is important to consider and design how to find potential customers for each product.

1. **Targeting and Market Segmentation:** Firstly, it's essential to identify the target customer base for each cloud product and conduct market segmentation analysis. Understanding the differences in requirements among different types of enterprises helps pinpoint the industries, sizes, and regions most likely to benefit from the product.

2. **Education and Awareness Building:** Cloud products typically require users to have a certain level of technical understanding. Thus, during customer acquisition, emphasis should be placed on education and raising awareness. This can be achieved through webinars, tutorial videos, technical documentation, etc., to impart product knowledge and usage methods to potential customers.

3. **Content Marketing and Professional Forums:** Utilize content marketing strategies to publish technical articles, case studies, customer success stories, etc., on professional forums, social media platforms, industry websites, etc. This helps attract the attention of target customers and builds a professional image.

4. **Partnership Relationships:** Establish close partnerships with industry peers to conduct joint marketing activities, host industry seminars or exhibitions, and expand the product's exposure and influence.

5. **Free Trials and Demonstrations:** Offer free trials or demo demonstrations to allow potential customers to experience the product's features and value firsthand, thereby increasing their confidence and interest.

6. **Personalized Marketing and Customer Guidance:** Develop personalized marketing plans based on customer characteristics and needs. Utilize targeted advertising, email marketing, customer relationship management tools, etc., for precise guidance and follow-up.

Customer acquisition for products in the cloud computing industry requires a tailored approach that considers industry characteristics and product features. Through targeted market positioning, content marketing, partnership relationships, and other means, potential customers can be effectively attracted and acquired. Continuous optimization and improvement of customer acquisition strategies ensure sustainable business growth and success.

3.1.1 Customer Segmentation

Segmenting customers allows CSPs to tailor their marketing efforts to specific groups with similar needs, preferences, and characteristics. By understanding the unique requirements of each segment, CSPs can create targeted messaging and campaigns that resonate with their intended audience, leading to higher engagement and conversion rates.

Different customer segments may have varying needs, priorities, and pain points. By segmenting customers, CSPs can develop customized offerings, pricing plans, and service packages that address the specific requirements of each segment. This helps enhance customer satisfaction and loyalty by delivering solutions that align closely with their business objectives.

Segmenting customers enables CSPs to allocate resources more effectively and efficiently. By prioritizing high-value segments or those with the greatest growth potential, CSPs can focus their sales, support, and product development efforts where they will have the most significant impact. This optimization of resources helps maximize ROI and profitability.

Understanding the distinct needs and preferences of different customer segments allows CSPs to deliver a more personalized and relevant customer experience. By tailoring their services, communications, and support to meet the specific requirements of each segment, CSPs can enhance satisfaction levels, drive loyalty, and foster long-term relationships with their customers.

Overall, effective customer segmentation enables CSPs to better understand their diverse customer base, optimize resource allocation, and deliver tailored solutions that drive customer satisfaction, loyalty, and business success in the highly competitive cloud services market.

Segmenting customers for cloud products involves dividing them into groups based on specific characteristics or dimensions that are relevant to the cloud service being offered. Some dimensions that can be used to segment customers for cloud products include:

1. **Industry Vertical:** Segmenting customers based on the industry they operate in, such as healthcare, finance, manufacturing, or technology. Different industries may have unique requirements and compliance standards that impact their cloud service needs.

2. **Company Size:** Segmenting customers based on the size of their organization, such as small and medium-sized businesses (SMBs) versus large enterprises. Company size can influence factors like budget, scalability requirements, and IT infrastructure complexity.

3. **Geographic Location:** Segmenting customers based on their geographic location, such as country, region, or proximity to data centers. Geographic factors may impact latency, data sovereignty requirements, and regulatory compliance.

4. **Usage Patterns:** Segmenting customers based on their usage patterns and resource consumption levels. This could include factors like frequency of usage, volume of data processed or stored, and types of workloads deployed.

5. **Technical Sophistication:** Segmenting customers based on their technical expertise and requirements. Some customers may require advanced features, customization options, or integration capabilities, while others may prefer simplicity and ease of use.

6. **Budget and Spending Capacity:** Segmenting customers based on their budget constraints and spending capacity. This could include categories such as high-spending enterprise customers, cost-conscious SMBs, or customers with fluctuating budgetary needs.

7. **Stage of Adoption:** Segmenting customers based on their stage of adoption of cloud technologies, such as early adopters, mainstream users, or laggards. Different segments may have varying levels of familiarity with cloud services and readiness to adopt new technologies.

8. **Customer Behavior:** Segmenting customers based on their behavior, such as purchase history, engagement with the platform, support interactions, and feedback. Understanding customer behavior can help tailor marketing efforts, improve customer retention, and identify upsell opportunities.

9. **Compliance and Security Requirements:** Segmenting customers based on their compliance and security requirements, such as industry regulations (e.g., HIPAA for healthcare) or data protection standards (e.g., GDPR). Customers in regulated industries may have unique needs for data protection and compliance support.

10. **Customer Goals and Objectives:** Segmenting customers based on their business goals, objectives, and use cases for cloud services. This could include factors like digital transformation initiatives, innovation priorities, or specific business challenges they are looking to address.

By analyzing and segmenting customers along these dimensions, CSPs can better understand their diverse customer base, tailor their offerings to meet specific needs, and provide personalized solutions and services that drive value for their customers.

3.1.2 Content Marketing

Content marketing is a strategic marketing approach focused on creating and distributing valuable, relevant, and consistent content to attract and engage a target audience. Rather than directly promoting a product or service, content marketing aims to provide valuable information, entertainment, or education to consumers, thereby building trust, credibility, and brand awareness over time.

Cloud products often involve complex technologies and services. Content marketing allows cloud service providers (CSPs) to educate potential customers about the benefits, features, and use cases of their offerings. By providing informative content such as blog posts, whitepapers, and tutorials, CSPs can help potential customers understand how cloud products can address their specific needs and challenges.

Trust is crucial in the cloud industry, where customers rely on CSPs to securely manage their data and applications. Content marketing allows CSPs to establish themselves as industry leaders and experts by sharing valuable insights, case studies, and best practices. By consistently delivering high-quality content, CSPs can build trust and credibility with their target audience.

Content marketing can drive lead generation and conversions for cloud products by attracting potential customers through informative and engaging content. By addressing common pain points and providing solutions, CSPs can capture the interest of potential customers and guide them through the buyer's journey, ultimately leading to conversions.

Content marketing is not only about acquiring new customers but also about supporting existing customers throughout their journey. By providing ongoing educational resources, best practices, and product updates, CSPs can help customers maximize the value of their cloud investments and achieve their business goals.

Overall, content marketing plays a crucial role in driving awareness, engagement, and conversions for cloud products. By delivering valuable and relevant content, CSPs can educate, inspire, and ultimately win the trust of their target audience, leading to long-term success in the competitive cloud market.

Content marketing for cloud and AI products requires a strategic approach to effectively engage with target audiences and drive conversions. Here are some steps to execute a successful content marketing strategy for these products:

1. **Understand Your Audience:** Begin by conducting thorough research to understand your target audience's needs, pain points, interests, and preferences. Identify key demographics, industries, and roles that are likely to benefit from your cloud and AI products. This is the outcome of the customer segmentation work described in the previous section of this book.

2. **Create Buyer Personas:** Develop detailed buyer personas based on your research findings. These personas should represent your ideal customers and include information such as job title, responsibilities, challenges, goals, preferred content formats, and buying behavior.

3. **Define Your Value Proposition:** Clearly articulate the unique value proposition of your cloud and AI products. What specific problems do they solve? What benefits do they offer? How do they differentiate from competitors? Use this information to shape your content messaging and positioning.

4. **Develop a Content Strategy:** Based on your audience insights and value proposition, create a content strategy that aligns with your marketing objectives. Determine the types of content you will create (e.g., blog posts, case studies, whitepapers, videos, webinars) and the topics you will cover. Consider incorporating a mix of educational, promotional, and thought leadership content.

5. **Produce High-Quality Content:** Create compelling and informative content that resonates with your target audience. Ensure that your content is well-researched, engaging, and relevant to your audience's interests and needs. Use

MONETIZE CLOUD & AI

visuals, storytelling, and data-driven insights to enhance the effectiveness of your content.

6. **Optimize for SEO:** Optimize your content for search engines to increase visibility and attract organic traffic. Conduct keyword research to identify relevant keywords and incorporate them naturally into your content. Pay attention to on-page SEO elements such as title tags, meta descriptions, headings, and internal linking.

7. **Promote Your Content:** Use a multi-channel approach to distribute and promote your content across various platforms and channels. This may include your website, blog, social media channels, email newsletters, industry forums, and guest blogging opportunities. Tailor your messaging and distribution strategy to each platform to maximize reach and engagement.

8. **Engage with Your Audience:** Actively engage with your audience by responding to comments, questions, and feedback on your content. Encourage discussions, foster community interaction, and build relationships with your audience members. This will help you establish credibility, trust, and loyalty among your target audience.

9. **Measure and Analyze Performance:** Track the performance of your content marketing efforts using key metrics such as website traffic, engagement metrics (e.g., likes, shares, comments), lead generation, and conversion rates. Use analytics tools to gain insights into what content resonates most with your audience and adjust your strategy accordingly.

10. **Iterate and Improve:** Continuously evaluate and refine your content marketing strategy based on performance

data and audience feedback. Experiment with different content formats, topics, and distribution channels to identify what works best for your target audience. By continuously iterating and improving your approach, you can optimize the effectiveness of your content marketing efforts over time.

3.1.3 Freemium Strategy

The "Freemium" strategy is a business model where a company offers both free and premium versions of its product or service.

The basic version, typically referred to as "free," provides limited features or functionality at no cost to the user. Users can then choose to upgrade to the premium version, which offers additional features or capabilities, often for a subscription fee. The goal of the freemium strategy is to attract users with the free offering and encourage them to upgrade to the premium version for access to more advanced or exclusive features.

Freemium models allow cloud and AI products to penetrate the market more effectively by removing barriers to entry. This enables a wider audience to access the product and increases its visibility. Offering a free version of the product attracts more users who may later convert to paying customers as they become familiar with the product's value and features.

Users can try out the basic features of the product before committing to a paid plan. This gives them an opportunity to evaluate its usefulness and suitability for their needs. Freemium models provide opportunities to upsell premium features or additional services to users who require more advanced functionality or support.

Also, having a large user base using the free version can provide valuable feedback for product improvement and feature development.

This feedback loop helps in enhancing the product to better meet customer needs.

Designing a freemium mechanism for cloud and AI products involves careful consideration of various factors to ensure it effectively attracts users, provides value, and encourages conversion to paid plans. Here's a step-by-step approach:

1. **Define Freemium Model**: Determine the features and functionalities that will be offered for free and those reserved for paid plans. This could include limitations on usage, storage, or access to advanced features.

2. **Create Compelling Free Tier**: Design the free version of your product to provide enough value to users while leaving room for upselling to premium plans. Ensure that the free tier addresses key pain points and showcases the product's capabilities.

3. **Implement Usage Limits**: Define usage limits for the free tier, such as the number of users, data storage, processing power, or features available. These limits should encourage users to upgrade to paid plans as their needs grow.

4. **Offer Upgrade Pathways**: Clearly communicate the benefits of upgrading to a paid plan, such as access to premium features, increased storage or performance, priority support, and enhanced security. Provide seamless pathways for users to upgrade within the product interface.

5. **Provide Onboarding and Support**: Offer comprehensive onboarding materials, tutorials, and documentation to help users get started with the free version of the product. Provide responsive customer support to address any questions or issues users may encounter.

6. **Monitor and Iterate**: Continuously monitor user engagement, conversion rates, and feedback to identify areas for improvement. Iterate on the freemium model based on user behavior and market trends to optimize conversion rates and customer satisfaction.

7. **Optimize Conversion Funnel**: Implement strategies to encourage conversion from free to paid plans, such as limited-time offers, discounts, or exclusive features for upgraded users. Test different pricing tiers, messaging, and incentives to optimize the conversion funnel.

By following these steps and regularly refining your freemium strategy based on user feedback and market insights, you can effectively design a freemium mechanism that attracts users, drives engagement, and maximizes revenue for your cloud and AI products.

3.1.4 Customer Nurturing

Customer nurturing refers to the process of building and maintaining relationships with potential and existing customers by providing them with valuable content, personalized experiences, and ongoing support at every stage of their journey. The goal of customer nurturing is to guide individuals through the buying cycle, from initial awareness to conversion and beyond, fostering trust, loyalty, and advocacy along the way.

Customer nurturing is particularly important for cloud and AI products due to their complex nature and the long-term relationships they entail.

The sales cycles for cloud and AI products can be lengthy, involving multiple touchpoints and stakeholders. Customer nurturing keeps prospects engaged throughout the process, guiding them through each stage of the journey and preventing drop-offs.

Nurturing existing customers can also lead to opportunities for upselling and cross-selling additional products or services. By understanding customers' evolving needs and preferences, businesses can identify opportunities to expand their offerings and increase revenue.

Here is key points to execute a fruitful customer nurturing mechanism:

- Develop high-quality, relevant content that addresses the needs and interests of your audience segments. This can include blog posts, articles, videos, webinars, case studies, whitepapers, and infographics. Focus on providing value and solving problems for your audience.

- Engage with your audience across multiple channels and touchpoints, including email marketing, social media, website content, events, and customer support. Use an integrated approach to create a consistent and cohesive experience across all channels.

- Implement lead nurturing campaigns to guide leads through the buyer's journey from awareness to purchase. Use marketing automation tools to deliver personalized content and messages based on lead behavior and preferences.

- Personalize your communications and interactions based on individual customer data, such as past interactions, preferences, and purchase history. Use dynamic content, personalized recommendations, and targeted messaging to create relevant experiences for each customer.

3.2 Customer Onboarding

Customer onboarding refers to the process of integrating and familiarizing new customers with a product or service. It involves guiding customers through the initial steps of using a product or service, providing them with the necessary resources and support to ensure a smooth transition, and helping them derive value from their investment.

Customer onboarding typically includes activities such as account setup, product demonstrations, training sessions, and ongoing support to address any questions or issues that may arise. The goal of customer onboarding is to ensure a positive first impression, establish a strong foundation for the customer relationship, and ultimately drive customer satisfaction and retention.

Cloud and AI products often involve complex technologies and functionalities. Customer onboarding needs to focus on providing comprehensive training and education to help users understand the capabilities of the product and how to leverage them effectively.

Cloud and AI products may need to integrate with existing systems or workflows within an organization. Effective onboarding involves guiding customers through the integration process, addressing any compatibility issues, and ensuring seamless integration with minimal disruption to existing operations.

Additionally, due to the nature of cloud and AI products being primarily delivered over the internet, it's essential to provide online onboarding processes and capabilities. This allows customers to independently create accounts and begin using the product, which is crucial for their convenience and satisfaction.

The number of steps involved in onboarding a customer online for a cloud product can vary depending on the complexity of the product and the specific requirements of the service provider. However, a typical onboarding process may include the following steps:

1. **Account Creation:** The customer creates an account by providing necessary information such as name, email address, and password.

2. **Verification:** The customer verifies their email address or phone number to confirm their identity.

3. **Profile Setup:** The customer completes their profile by providing additional details such as company name, contact information, and preferences.

4. **Payment Setup:** The customer enters payment details to set up billing for the selected subscription plan.

5. **Configuration:** The customer configures the cloud product according to their requirements, such as setting up user permissions, defining workflows, or integrating with other systems.

6. **Onboarding Resources:** The customer is provided with resources, tutorials, or guides to help them get started with using the cloud product effectively.

7. **Training or Demo:** Optionally, the customer may receive training sessions or product demos to learn about advanced features or best practices.

8. **Support Access:** The customer gains access to customer support channels for assistance or troubleshooting during the onboarding process and beyond.

9. **Welcome Communication:** The customer receives a welcome email or message that summarizes the onboarding process and provides further instructions or next steps.

These steps can be adjusted or expanded based on the specific requirements of the cloud product and the preferences of the service provider.

3.2.1 Customer Account

A customer account for a Cloud Service Provider (CSP) is a digital record or profile maintained by the CSP that contains information about an individual or organization that is using the cloud services provided by the CSP. This account serves as the gateway for customers to access and manage various cloud services and resources offered by the provider.

Key features and components of a customer account typically include:

1. **Account Information**: Basic details such as the customer's name, email address, contact information, and organization details.

2. **Authentication Credentials**: Username, password, and any additional authentication methods used to secure access to the account.

3. **Subscription Details**: Information about the customer's subscription plan or service tier, including billing details and payment methods.

4. **Usage and Billing History**: Records of the customer's usage of cloud services and billing history, including invoices, payment receipts, and usage reports.

5. **Resource Management**: Tools and interfaces for managing cloud resources, such as virtual machines, storage, databases, and networking components.

6. **Security Settings**: Configuration options for security features such as access controls, encryption settings, and identity management.

7. **Support and Communication**: Access to customer support channels, help documentation, and communication preferences for receiving updates and notifications from the CSP.

Customer accounts are essential for facilitating the provisioning, management, and support of cloud services, enabling customers to effectively utilize and benefit from the offerings provided by the CSP.

Designing a smooth function for customers to create an account in a CSP portal involves considering several key aspects to ensure a seamless and user-friendly experience. Here are some steps to achieve this:

1. **Simple Registration Process**: Keep the registration process simple and intuitive. Only ask for essential information upfront, such as name, email address, and password. Additional details can be collected later.

2. **Clear Call-to-Action**: Provide a clear and prominent "Sign Up" or "Create Account" button on the portal's homepage or landing page to encourage users to begin the registration process.

3. **Progress Indicators**: If the registration process involves multiple steps, use progress indicators to show users how far they are in completing the process and what steps are remaining.

4. **Mobile-Friendly Design**: Ensure that the registration process is optimized for mobile devices, as many users may prefer to sign up using smartphones or tablets.

5. **Real-Time Validation**: Implement real-time validation for user inputs to catch errors early and provide immediate feedback to users if there are any issues with the information they entered.

6. **Social Sign-Up Options**: Offer the option for users to sign up using their existing social media accounts (e.g., Google, Facebook, LinkedIn) to streamline the registration process and reduce friction.

7. **Email Verification**: After users submit their registration information, send a verification email with a unique link to confirm their email address and activate their account.

8. **Guided Tour or Tutorial**: Consider providing a guided tour or tutorial to walk users through the registration process, especially if it involves complex steps or features.

9. **Clear Privacy Policy and Terms of Service**: Provide links to your privacy policy and terms of service during the registration process, and ensure that users understand how their information will be used and protected.

10. **Error Handling and Recovery**: Anticipate and handle common registration errors gracefully, providing clear error messages and guidance on how to correct them. Allow users to easily recover from any errors without losing their progress.

11. **Optional Profile Completion**: Allow users to skip optional profile completion steps during registration and complete them later from their account settings.

By following these guidelines and best practices, you can design a smooth and user-friendly account creation function for your CSP portal, improving the overall user experience and encouraging more users to sign up for your services.

3.2.2 Customer Verification

Customer verification for a CSP (Cloud Service Provider) involves confirming the identity and authenticity of customers who sign up for their services. This process ensures that the individuals or organizations accessing the cloud services are legitimate and authorized users.

Verifying the identity of customers helps prevent unauthorized access to cloud services, protecting sensitive data and resources stored on the platform. It reduces the risk of security breaches, data theft, and cyber attacks.

And also, many industries are subject to regulatory requirements regarding customer identity verification, such as Know Your Customer (KYC) and anti-money laundering (AML) regulations. CSPs must comply with these regulations to avoid legal penalties and reputational damage.

Implementing robust customer verification measures instills trust and confidence in the CSP's platform among customers and stakeholders. It demonstrates the CSP's commitment to security, compliance, and protecting user data, enhancing its reputation in the market.

Customer verification typically includes several steps:

1. **Identity Verification**: Customers may be required to provide official identification documents, such as government-issued IDs, passports, or driver's licenses, to confirm their identity.

2. **Contact Information Verification**: Customers must provide valid contact information, including email addresses and phone numbers, which are verified to ensure they are reachable.

3. **Address Verification**: Some CSPs may require customers to verify their physical address by providing utility bills or other official documents.

4. **Business Verification (for organizations)**: In the case of organizational customers, additional verification steps may be necessary to confirm the legitimacy of the business, such as providing business licenses, tax identification numbers, or corporate registration documents.

5. **Payment Verification**: Customers may need to verify their payment information, such as credit card details or bank account information, to complete the registration process and enable billing for the cloud services.

6. **Authentication**: After verification, customers may need to authenticate their identity each time they access the CSP's services, typically through the use of passwords, two-factor authentication (2FA), or other security measures.

Integrating with third-party identity verification services allows CSPs to validate customer identities more thoroughly. These services typically use a variety of data sources, such as government-issued IDs, credit reports, and biometric data, to verify the identity of individuals. By leveraging these services, CSPs can improve the accuracy and reliability of their customer verification process.

Third-party data enrichment platforms provide CSPs with access to additional data sources that can enrich customer profiles and improve the accuracy of identity verification. These platforms aggregate data from various public and private sources, such as social media profiles, property records, and financial databases, to provide a more comprehensive view of customers.

3.2.3 Customer Organization

For customers of cloud computing products, most are enterprises, government agencies, research institutions, and other large organizations. Many of these organizations comprise multiple subsidiaries, departments, or lower-level units that may need to purchase cloud products from the same CSP (Cloud Service Provider). Therefore, for CSPs, it is not sufficient to abstract these organizations as a single customer entity. Instead, they need to provide organization information management capabilities that match their actual situations. This management capability should be integrated with customer information authentication, contract signing, product ordering, discount application, bill splitting, and other business processes to ensure effective management and service delivery to these complex organizational structures.

Managing a customer's organization for a Cloud Service Provider (CSP) involves several key steps:

1. **Organizational Structure Mapping**: Understand the customer's organizational hierarchy, including subsidiaries, departments, and other relevant units.

2. **Organization Information Collection**: Gather comprehensive information about each entity within the customer's organization, including contact details, roles, responsibilities, and requirements.

3. **Centralized Database**: Establish a centralized database or CRM system to store and manage organization-related

information. This database should provide a unified view of the entire organizational structure.

4. **Customized Organization Profiles**: Create customized organization profiles for each entity, allowing for easy access to relevant information and preferences.

5. **Access Control**: Implement access control mechanisms to ensure that only authorized personnel can view and modify organization-related data.

6. **Integration with Business Processes**: Integrate organization management capabilities with various business processes such as customer authentication, contract management, product ordering, billing, and support.

7. **Regular Updates**: Regularly update organization profiles to reflect any changes in the customer's organizational structure or requirements.

8. **Security and Compliance**: Ensure that organization-related data is securely stored and managed in compliance with relevant regulations and data protection standards.

By effectively managing a customer's organization, CSPs can streamline operations, enhance customer satisfaction, and better tailor their services to meet the unique needs of each organizational unit.

3.3 Customer Communication

Customer communication refers to the exchange of information between a business and its customers. This communication can take various forms, including emails, phone calls, social media interactions, chat support, newsletters, and more. It encompasses all interactions aimed at providing customers with relevant information, addressing their concerns or inquiries, and building a relationship with them. Effective customer communication is crucial for building trust, loyalty, and satisfaction, ultimately leading to customer retention and business success.

Customer communication throughout the entire customer lifecycle is essential for fostering positive relationships, addressing customer needs, and maximizing customer satisfaction. Here's how customer communication can be structured across different stages of the customer lifecycle in the cloud and AI industry:

1. **Awareness Stage:**

   • Content Marketing: Use blogs, articles, whitepapers, and social media to educate potential customers about the benefits of cloud and AI solutions.

   • Webinars and Events: Host webinars, workshops, and industry events to showcase your products/services and engage with prospects.

2. **Consideration Stage:**

   • Email Campaigns: Send targeted emails to prospects with relevant content, case studies, and testimonials to help them evaluate your offerings.

   • Demo Requests: Encourage prospects to schedule product demos or trials to experience the benefits firsthand.

   • Sales Calls: Conduct personalized sales calls to address specific questions or concerns and guide prospects through the decision-making process.

3. Purchase Stage:

- Transparent Pricing: Clearly communicate pricing plans, discounts, and promotions to facilitate the purchase decision.

- Contract Negotiation: Provide clear terms and conditions, and ensure smooth contract negotiation and signing processes.

- Onboarding Materials: Deliver onboarding materials, such as welcome emails, setup guides, and tutorials, to help new customers get started quickly.

4. Implementation Stage:

- Dedicated Support: Assign dedicated account managers or support representatives to assist customers during the implementation phase.

- Training Sessions: Offer training sessions, webinars, or online courses to help customers learn how to use the product effectively.

- Regular Updates: Keep customers informed about product updates, enhancements, and best practices for maximizing value.

5. Utilization Stage:

- Proactive Support: Monitor customer usage patterns and proactively reach out to offer assistance or guidance when needed.

- Knowledge Base: Maintain a comprehensive knowledge base or FAQ section where customers can find answers to common questions and troubleshoot issues on their own.

- Community Forums: Foster a community where customers can share experiences, tips, and best practices with each other.

6. Renewal/Expansion Stage:

- Renewal Reminders: Send timely reminders about upcoming renewals and provide incentives or discounts for renewing subscriptions.

- Upselling/Cross-Selling: Identify opportunities for upselling or cross-selling additional products or services based on customer needs and usage patterns.

- Customer Success Reviews: Conduct regular check-ins or reviews with customers to assess satisfaction, address concerns, and identify opportunities for expansion.

7. Retention/Advocacy Stage:

- Customer Feedback Surveys: Gather feedback through surveys or interviews to understand customer satisfaction levels and areas for improvement.

- Referral Programs: Encourage satisfied customers to refer others to your products/services through referral programs or incentives.

- Customer Success Stories: Showcase success stories and testimonials from satisfied customers to build trust and credibility with prospects.

By implementing a comprehensive customer communication strategy throughout the entire customer lifecycle, cloud and AI companies can effectively engage customers, drive adoption, and foster long-term relationships that lead to advocacy and growth.

3.3.1 Digital Channel

Digital channels such as email, social media, websites, and mobile apps are accessible anytime, anywhere, allowing customers to interact with companies at their convenience and playing a crucial role in customer communication in the cloud and AI industry for several reasons:

1. **Reach:** Digital channels have a vast reach, enabling companies to connect with a global audience of potential and existing customers regardless of geographical boundaries.

2. **Cost-Effectiveness:** Compared to traditional communication channels like phone calls or direct mail, digital channels often have lower costs, making them an efficient and cost-effective way to communicate with customers, especially at scale.

3. **Personalization:** Digital channels offer opportunities for personalization through targeted messaging, content customization, and behavioral tracking, allowing companies to tailor communications to individual customer preferences and interests.

4. **Real-Time Engagement:** Digital channels enable real-time engagement, allowing companies to respond to customer inquiries, provide support, and deliver relevant information promptly, enhancing the overall customer experience.

5. **Data Analytics:** Digital channels provide valuable data and analytics insights into customer behavior, preferences, and

engagement metrics. Companies can leverage this data to optimize their communication strategies, improve targeting, and measure the effectiveness of their campaigns.

6. **Integration:** Digital channels can be seamlessly integrated with other systems and technologies, such as customer relationship management (CRM) platforms, marketing automation tools, and analytics platforms, enabling companies to create cohesive and integrated customer communication experiences.

7. **Flexibility and Agility:** Digital channels offer flexibility and agility, allowing companies to quickly adapt and respond to changing market dynamics, customer needs, and emerging trends. This agility is essential in the fast-paced and constantly evolving cloud and AI industry.

Overall, digital channels provide an essential foundation for effective customer communication in the cloud and AI industry, enabling companies to engage with customers across various touchpoints, drive engagement and loyalty, and ultimately drive business growth.

However, managing multiple digital channels separately can be cumbersome and inefficient. By consolidating channels, companies can streamline their communication efforts, centralize management, and allocate resources more effectively.

Furthermore, consolidating digital channels allows companies to provide a unified and consistent customer experience across all touchpoints. When customers interact with a company through different channels, they expect seamless transitions and consistent messaging regardless of the channel they use.

Consolidating digital channels enables companies to aggregate and integrate customer data from various sources. This unified data repository provides a comprehensive view of customer interactions and behavior, allowing companies to gain valuable insights and personalize communication more effectively.

With multiple digital channels operating independently, it can be challenging to analyze and derive insights from scattered data sources. Consolidating channels simplifies data analysis, facilitates cross-channel analytics, and enables companies to measure the effectiveness of their communication strategies more accurately. A consolidated approach to digital communication enables companies to develop a holistic communication strategy that aligns with their overall business objectives. This allows for better coordination of messaging, branding, and customer engagement initiatives across channels.

3.3.2 Communication History

The communication history for a customer of a CSP (Cloud Service Provider) refers to a record or log of all interactions and communications between the customer and the CSP across various channels and touchpoints.

Keeping track of communication history allows CSP representatives to provide personalized and efficient customer service. They can quickly access past interactions, understand customer preferences, and resolve issues more effectively, leading to higher customer satisfaction.

By maintaining a record of previous communications, CSPs ensure continuity of support across different channels and touchpoints. Customers don't have to repeat their concerns or provide redundant information, leading to a smoother support experience.

Communication history provides transparency into the customer-provider relationship. It allows both parties to refer to previous agreements, discussions, or commitments, reducing misunderstandings and fostering trust.

In some cases, maintaining communication history may be necessary for legal or compliance reasons. It ensures that CSPs have a documented trail of interactions in case of disputes, regulatory inquiries, or audits.

Communication history can provide valuable insights into customer behavior, preferences, and needs. Analyzing this data can help CSPs identify trends, anticipate customer requirements, and tailor their offerings and services accordingly.

Overall, managing communication history is essential for delivering exceptional customer experiences, maintaining accountability and transparency, meeting regulatory requirements, and driving continuous improvement in CSP operations.

Implementing an effective communication history management mechanism for a CSP involves several key steps:

1. **Selecting Communication Channels:** Identify and integrate the various communication channels used by the CSP, such as email, chat, phone calls, social media, and support tickets. Ensure compatibility and seamless integration between these channels.

2. **Deploying a Customer Relationship Management (CRM) System:** Implement a robust CRM system that can centralize and organize communication history data. Choose a CRM platform that offers features specifically designed for managing customer interactions and histories.

3. **Capturing Interaction Data:** Configure the CRM system to automatically capture and record all customer interactions across different channels. This includes details such as

communication timestamps, channel used, customer queries, resolutions provided, and any follow-up actions taken.

4. **Organizing and Categorizing Data:** Develop a standardized system for organizing and categorizing communication history data within the CRM platform. Use tags, labels, or categories to classify interactions based on factors like customer type, issue category, priority level, and resolution status.

5. **Ensuring Data Integrity and Security:** Implement measures to ensure the integrity and security of communication history data. This includes encryption protocols, access controls, audit trails, and regular data backups to prevent unauthorized access, tampering, or loss of information.

6. **Enabling Cross-Channel Visibility:** Enable cross-channel visibility within the CRM system, allowing customer service representatives to access and view complete communication histories regardless of the channel used. This ensures consistent and coherent support across all touchpoints.

7. **Facilitating Search and Retrieval:** Implement robust search and retrieval functionalities within the CRM system, enabling users to quickly locate and access specific communication records based on keywords, dates, customer identifiers, or other criteria.

8. **Integrating with Analytics and Reporting Tools:** Integrate the CRM system with analytics and reporting tools to gain insights from communication history data. Analyze trends, identify patterns, track performance metrics, and generate reports to measure the effectiveness of customer communication strategies.

9. **Training and Empowering Staff:** Provide comprehensive training to customer service representatives on how to effectively use the CRM system for managing communication history. Empower them with the knowledge and tools needed to access, interpret, and leverage communication data to enhance customer interactions.

3.3.3 Personalize Communication

Personalized communication refers to the practice of tailoring messages, content, and interactions to individual recipients based on their specific preferences, behaviors, demographics, and past interactions. Rather than delivering generic, one-size-fits-all communications, personalized communication aims to create more relevant and engaging experiences for each recipient.

Personalized communication can be implemented across various channels and touchpoints, including email marketing, website content, mobile apps, social media, and customer support interactions. By delivering messages that are tailored to individual preferences and needs, organizations can foster stronger relationships with their audience, drive engagement and loyalty, and ultimately improve business outcomes.

Implementing personalized communication in the cloud and AI industry involves leveraging data, technology, and best practices to tailor messages and interactions to individual users. Here are steps to implement personalized communication effectively:

1. **Collect Relevant Data**: Gather data from various sources, including user interactions with your platform, demographic information, past purchases, preferences, and behavior. Ensure data privacy and compliance with regulations.

2. **Segmentation**: Analyze the collected data to segment users into groups with similar characteristics or behaviors. Common segmentation criteria include demographics, usage patterns, engagement levels, and lifecycle stage.

3. **Develop Customer Profiles**: Create detailed customer profiles based on the segmented data. Include information such as user preferences, purchase history, browsing behavior, and communication preferences.

4. **Personalize Content**: Tailor messages, recommendations, and content based on the customer profiles. Use dynamic content generation to deliver personalized product recommendations, promotions, and offers.

5. **Automation**: Implement marketing automation tools to deliver personalized messages at scale. Use triggers and workflows to send automated messages based on user actions, such as abandoned carts, completed purchases, or milestone achievements.

6. **Omni-Channel Approach**: Engage users across multiple channels, including email, SMS, in-app notifications, social media, and website content. Ensure consistency and coherence in messaging across all channels.

7. **A/B Testing**: Experiment with different message variations and content formats to identify what resonates best with different segments of your audience. Use A/B testing to optimize message effectiveness and engagement rates.

8. **Real-Time Personalization**: Utilize real-time data to personalize experiences in the moment. For example, dynamically adjust website content or offer personalized

recommendations based on user behavior during their current session.

9. **Feedback Loop**: Encourage user feedback and actively listen to customer responses. Use feedback to refine your personalized communication strategy and improve customer experiences over time.

10. **Analytics and Optimization**: Measure the performance of your personalized communication efforts using relevant metrics such as open rates, click-through rates, conversion rates, and customer satisfaction scores. Use analytics to identify areas for improvement and optimize your strategy accordingly.

By following these steps and continuously refining your approach based on user feedback and analytics, you can effectively implement personalized communication strategies in the cloud and AI industry to enhance user engagement, drive customer satisfaction, and ultimately achieve your business objectives.

3.4 Loyalty and Retention

Customer loyalty and retention refer to the efforts made by a business to maintain and strengthen its relationship with existing customers, encouraging them to continue purchasing products or services over time.

Customer loyalty is the result of positive experiences, satisfaction, and trust that a customer has developed with a brand over time. Loyal customers are more likely to make repeat purchases, choose the brand over competitors, and advocate for the brand to others. Loyalty programs, excellent customer service, and consistent product quality are common strategies for fostering customer loyalty.

Customer retention focuses on keeping existing customers engaged and satisfied to prevent them from switching to competitors. It involves ongoing efforts to understand customer needs, address concerns, and provide value-added services to maintain their loyalty. Retention strategies may include personalized communication, special offers, loyalty rewards, and proactive customer support.

Both customer loyalty and retention are critical for the long-term success of a business, as acquiring new customers is typically more expensive than retaining existing ones. By cultivating loyalty and prioritizing retention efforts, businesses can benefit from increased customer lifetime value, higher revenue, and positive word-of-mouth referrals.

Many cloud products operate on a subscription-based model, where customers pay regularly for access to the service. This ongoing relationship requires a focus on continuously delivering value to customers to justify their continued subscription. Customer loyalty is closely tied to the perceived value of the service relative to its cost.

Cloud services are often characterized by low switching costs, meaning customers can easily switch between providers if they are dissatisfied. This makes customer retention particularly challenging, as providers must consistently deliver exceptional service and value to keep customers from exploring alternatives.

Cloud products generate vast amounts of data on customer usage patterns, behaviors, and preferences. Analyzing this data can provide valuable insights into customer needs and sentiments, enabling providers to personalize their offerings, improve the user experience, and proactively address issues that may impact loyalty and retention.

Despite the digital nature of cloud services, building strong relationships with customers remains essential for loyalty and retention. This involves proactive communication, personalized interactions, and responsive support to foster trust, satisfaction, and advocacy among customers.

In summary, customer loyalty and retention for cloud products require a proactive approach that emphasizes delivering ongoing value, leveraging data-driven insights, providing flexibility and scalability, fostering innovation, and building strong relationships with customers to maintain their loyalty in a competitive market.

3.4.1 Customer Loyalty

Measuring customer loyalty in the cloud and AI industry involves assessing various factors that indicate the strength of the relationship between customers and the service provider. Here are some key metrics and methods for measuring customer loyalty in this industry:

1. **Net Promoter Score (NPS)**: NPS measures the likelihood of customers to recommend a product or service to others. Customers are asked to rate their likelihood to recommend on a scale of 0 to 10. Those who give a score of 9 or 10 are considered promoters, while those who give a score of 6 or below are detractors. Subtracting the percentage of detractors from the percentage of promoters yields the NPS.

2. **Customer Satisfaction (CSAT)**: CSAT measures the satisfaction level of customers with a specific interaction or experience, such as a support ticket resolution or product feature. Customers are asked to rate their satisfaction on a scale, typically from 1 to 5 or 1 to 10.

3. **Churn Rate**: Churn rate measures the percentage of customers who stop using or subscribing to a service over a specific period. A high churn rate indicates low customer loyalty, while a low churn rate suggests that customers are satisfied and likely to continue using the service.

4. **Retention Rate**: Retention rate measures the percentage of customers who continue to use or subscribe to the service over time. It is the inverse of churn rate and reflects the ability of the company to retain its customer base.

5. **Repeat Purchase Rate**: For subscription-based services, repeat purchase rate measures the frequency with which customers renew their subscriptions or make additional purchases. A high repeat purchase rate indicates strong customer loyalty and satisfaction.

6. **Customer Feedback and Reviews**: Gathering feedback directly from customers through surveys, reviews, and testimonials can provide valuable insights into their satisfaction, loyalty, and areas for improvement.

By tracking and analyzing these metrics, cloud and AI service providers can gain a comprehensive understanding of customer loyalty and identify areas for improvement to enhance the overall customer experience and retention.

Improving customer loyalty in the cloud and AI industry requires a strategic approach focused on delivering exceptional customer experiences, building trust, and providing ongoing value. Here are some effective strategies to enhance customer loyalty:

1. **Deliver Outstanding Customer Service**: Provide responsive, knowledgeable, and personalized customer support to address inquiries, resolve issues promptly, and exceed customer expectations.

2. **Focus on Product Quality and Reliability**: Ensure that your cloud and AI products are reliable, user-friendly, and deliver on their promises. Continuously innovate and update

your offerings to stay ahead of the competition and meet evolving customer needs.

3. **Build Trust and Transparency**: Be transparent about your products, pricing, and policies. Establish trust by prioritizing data security, privacy, and compliance with regulations such as GDPR and CCPA.

4. **Create Loyalty Programs and Incentives**: Reward loyal customers with exclusive benefits, discounts, or rewards programs to incentivize continued engagement and repeat business.

5. **Solicit and Act on Customer Feedback**: Regularly seek feedback from customers through surveys, reviews, and feedback mechanisms. Use this input to identify areas for improvement and implement changes to address customer pain points and enhance the overall experience.

6. **Stay Responsive and Adaptive**: Stay attuned to market trends, emerging technologies, and customer needs. Continuously adapt and innovate your offerings to stay relevant and meet evolving customer expectations.

7. **Measure and Monitor Loyalty Metrics**: Regularly track key loyalty metrics such as NPS, CSAT, churn rate, and retention rate to gauge the effectiveness of your loyalty initiatives and identify areas for improvement.

By implementing these strategies, cloud and AI service providers can cultivate strong relationships with their customers, foster loyalty, and drive long-term success in a competitive marketplace.

3.4.2 Customer Retention

Early Warning Systems

Recognizing a leaving customer is the first step in any effective customer retention strategy. By identifying customers who are at risk of leaving, companies can take proactive measures to address their concerns, offer solutions, and ultimately retain their business.

Implement early warning systems that use data analytics and machine learning to detect signs of potential churn. These systems can analyze customer behavior, usage patterns, and engagement metrics to identify at-risk customers.

Monitor changes in usage patterns, such as a decrease in activity, usage of specific features, or frequency of logins. Sudden drops in usage may indicate disengagement and potential churn.

Monitor billing and payment behavior, including late payments, failed payments, or downgrades in subscription plans. Financial indicators can indicate financial difficulties or dissatisfaction with the product.

Track customer interactions with support, sales, and account management teams. Increased interactions, especially related to cancellation inquiries or contract renegotiations, may indicate churn risk.

By closely monitoring these indicators and leveraging data-driven insights, cloud and AI companies can proactively identify customers at risk of leaving and take targeted actions to mitigate churn and retain valuable relationships.

Automated Alerts

Set up automated alerts to notify account managers or customer success teams when a customer exhibits behaviors indicative of churn. This allows teams to intervene promptly and engage with the customer to address any issues.

Set thresholds for each churn indicator to determine when an alert should be triggered. For example, you may set a threshold for inactive usage beyond a certain period or a decrease in engagement below a specific threshold.

Define escalation procedures for alerts that require immediate attention or follow-up. Specify who should be notified and the appropriate steps to take in response to each alert.

Integrate alerting systems with your CRM or customer database to ensure that alerts are logged and tracked alongside customer records. This allows for better visibility and follow-up on customer interactions.

By implementing a proactive alerting system for leaving customers, you can identify potential churn risks early and take proactive measures to retain valuable customers and maintain long-term relationships.

Engagement Outreach

Engaging with a churning customer involves understanding their concerns, addressing their issues, and offering solutions to retain their business.

Contact the customer promptly after identifying them as churning to demonstrate your proactive approach to customer retention. Use the customer's preferred communication channel, whether it's email, phone, or in-app messaging.

Start the conversation by expressing genuine concern for the customer's experience and understanding of their situation. Let them know that you value their business and want to address any issues they may be facing.

Allow the customer to voice their concerns and listen actively to understand their reasons for considering churn. Encourage them to share any challenges or frustrations they've encountered with your product or service.

Based on the customer's feedback and issues, offer personalized solutions to address their specific needs and concerns. This could involve troubleshooting technical issues, providing additional support or training, or offering discounts or incentives to encourage retention.

If necessary, be willing to negotiate terms or offer concessions to meet the customer's needs and retain their business. This could include adjusting pricing plans, extending trial periods, or providing custom solutions.

By engaging with churning customers in a proactive, empathetic, and solution-oriented manner, you can increase the likelihood of retaining their business and fostering long-term loyalty.

Customer Feedback

Solicit feedback from leaving customers to understand the reasons behind their decision to churn. Use this feedback to identify areas for improvement and make necessary changes to prevent future churn.

Reactivation Campaigns

Implement reactivation campaigns targeting churned customers to win them back. Offer special promotions or reintroduce them to updated product features that address their initial concerns.

3.4.3 Customer Retirement

"Customer retirement" typically refers to the process of intentionally discontinuing or phasing out a customer's account or relationship with a business. This could occur for various reasons, such as the customer's decision to stop using the product or service, their business closure, or their transition to a competitor's offering. Customer retirement may involve closing the customer's account, discontinuing services, transferring data or assets, and formally ending the business relationship. The goal of customer retirement is to manage the exit process smoothly while preserving the business's reputation and maintaining positive relations with the departing customer.

In the context of the cloud and AI industry, customer retirement carries specific considerations due to the nature of the services provided:

1. **Data Migration and Deletion:** Cloud and AI services often involve the storage and processing of large volumes of data. When a customer decides to retire their account, special attention must be given to migrating or securely deleting their data in compliance with data protection regulations.

2. **Integration Discontinuation:** Customers using cloud and AI services may have integrated these solutions with their existing infrastructure or applications. Retirement processes need to account for the discontinuation of these integrations and provide support or guidance for transitioning to alternative solutions.

3. **Subscription Cancellation:** Cloud services are often subscription-based, and the retirement process may involve canceling or transitioning subscription plans. Clear communication about billing cycles, refunds (if applicable),

and the cancellation process is crucial to ensure a positive customer experience.

4. **Continuity of Service:** Depending on the criticality of the services provided, customers may require continuity during the retirement process to avoid disruptions to their operations. Ensuring a seamless transition or providing temporary support can help mitigate any negative impact on the customer's business.

Designing a smooth customer retirement mechanism for a CSP (Cloud Service Provider) involves several key steps to ensure a seamless process for both the customer and the provider. Here's a guide on how to design such a mechanism:

1. **Clear Retirement Policy**: Establish a clear and transparent policy outlining the process for customer retirement. Include information about data deletion or migration, subscription cancellation, and any relevant timelines or requirements.

2. **Self-Service Options**: Provide self-service options for customers to initiate the retirement process. This could include an online portal or dashboard where customers can submit retirement requests and manage their account closure.

3. **Data Management Tools**: Offer tools and resources to assist customers in managing their data during retirement. This may involve data export functionality, guidance on data deletion best practices, or assistance with data migration to alternative solutions.

4. **Communication Channels**: Maintain open lines of communication with retiring customers through multiple channels such as email, phone, or live chat. Keep customers informed at every step of the retirement process, including

confirmation of retirement request receipt, status updates, and final closure notifications.

5. **Smooth Transition Planning**: Collaborate with customers to develop a transition plan that minimizes disruption to their operations. This may involve staggered retirement timelines, temporary service extensions, or assistance with transitioning to alternative solutions.

6. **Post-Retirement Follow-Up**: Conduct post-retirement follow-up to ensure customer satisfaction and address any lingering issues or concerns. Offer assistance with post-retirement tasks such as data retrieval or account closure confirmation.

By following these steps, CSPs can design a smooth and efficient customer retirement mechanism that prioritizes customer satisfaction while ensuring compliance with data protection regulations and industry standards.

3.4.4 Customer Lifetime Value

Customer Lifetime Value (CLV), also known as Customer Lifetime Revenue or Lifetime Value (LTV), is a metric that represents the total revenue or profit a customer is expected to generate over the entire duration of their relationship with a business. CLV is a valuable indicator of the long-term value that a customer brings to a company and is used by businesses to make strategic decisions regarding customer acquisition, retention, and marketing investments.

Many cloud and AI products operate on a subscription-based model where customers pay recurring fees for access to services. This model often results in predictable revenue streams over time, making CLV calculations more accurate and reliable.

Cloud and AI providers often have a diverse portfolio of products and services. CLV analysis can help identify opportunities for cross-selling or upselling additional offerings to existing customers, thereby increasing their lifetime value.

Given the competitive landscape of the cloud and AI industry, customer retention is paramount. CLV analysis can inform strategies for reducing churn and improving customer satisfaction, such as targeted marketing campaigns, personalized recommendations, and proactive customer support initiatives.

Many cloud and AI vendors aim to establish long-term partnerships with their clients, spanning multiple years or even decades. CLV provides insights into the potential profitability of these relationships and helps prioritize investments in customer success and relationship management initiatives.

A long-term contract can be important for improving Customer Lifetime Value (CLV) in the cloud industry. Longer contract terms can help mitigate the risk of customer churn or attrition. When customers are locked into a contract for an extended period, they are less likely to switch to a competitor or terminate the relationship prematurely. This stability can lead to higher CLV by extending the duration of the customer lifecycle and maximizing revenue potential.

Meanwhile, CSPs offer discounts or incentives for customers who commit to long-term contracts, such as reduced pricing or waived setup fees. These cost savings can incentivize customers to opt for longer contract terms, enhancing their perceived value proposition and increasing CLV by maximizing their return on investment.

4

ORDERING

In a competitive market, a seamless ordering process can be a key differentiator for a cloud provider. A user-friendly ordering system that is easy to navigate and understand can attract customers and help the provider stand out from the competition.

A smooth and efficient ordering process enhances customer satisfaction. Customers appreciate simplicity, clarity, and ease of use when placing orders for cloud services. A positive ordering experience can lead to customer loyalty and retention.

A complicated or frustrating ordering experience may lead to customer churn, where customers abandon the service in favor of competitors. By optimizing the ordering process and making it as frictionless as possible, cloud providers can reduce churn rates and retain more customers.

Ordering cloud products can be complex for several reasons:

- **Technical Complexity:** Cloud products often come with a wide range of technical features, configurations, and options. Understanding these technical aspects and selecting the right configurations to meet specific requirements can be challenging for users who may not have expertise in cloud technologies.

- **Customization:** Cloud products typically offer various customization options to cater to different user needs and preferences. Choosing the appropriate customization options while considering factors such as scalability, performance, security, and compliance adds complexity to the ordering process.

- **Integration Requirements:** Users may need to integrate cloud products with their existing infrastructure, applications, or workflows. Ensuring seamless integration and compatibility with other systems can require careful consideration of technical specifications and dependencies.

- **Cost Considerations:** Cloud pricing models can be complex, with factors such as usage-based pricing, tiered pricing, discounts, and additional fees. Understanding the cost implications of different configurations and usage patterns is essential for making informed decisions during the ordering process.

A well-designed ordering process can facilitate upselling and cross-selling opportunities. By presenting customers with relevant options and upgrades during the ordering process, cloud providers can increase their average order value and generate more revenue.

A good ordering system for a cloud service provider should encompass several key functionalities to ensure a smooth and efficient ordering process. Here's a functional framework outlining the essential components:

1. **Customizable Ordering Options:**

   - Provide flexible ordering options to accommodate various customer needs, such as on-demand, subscription-based, or pay-as-you-go models.

   - Allow customers to customize their orders by selecting desired configurations, resources, and features.

2. Real-Time Availability and Pricing:

- Display real-time availability and pricing information for cloud services based on current resource availability and market conditions.

- Ensure consistency and accuracy of pricing across different channels and customer segments.

3. Shopping Cart and Order Management:

- Allow customers to add multiple items to a shopping cart before proceeding to checkout.

- Enable customers to review and modify their orders before finalizing the purchase.

- Provide order tracking and status updates throughout the fulfillment process.

4. Integration with Billing and Payment Systems:

- Seamless integration with billing and invoicing systems to generate accurate bills based on ordered services and usage.

- Support multiple payment methods, including credit cards, bank transfers, and electronic wallets.

- Ensure compliance with security standards and regulations for handling payment information.

5. Automated Provisioning and Deployment:

- Automate the provisioning and deployment of ordered cloud services to minimize manual intervention and accelerate time-to-value for customers.

- Integrate with orchestration and configuration management tools to streamline resource allocation and setup.

6. Customer Support and Self-Service Tools:

- Provide access to self-service tools and resources to help customers troubleshoot issues, manage their accounts, and access support documentation.

- Offer multiple channels for customer support, such as live chat, email, and knowledge base articles.

7. Analytics and Reporting:

- Capture and analyze data on ordering trends, customer preferences, and conversion rates to optimize the ordering process and improve business outcomes.

- Generate reports and dashboards to track key metrics related to order volume, revenue, and customer satisfaction.

4.1 Order Configuration

Providing easy-to-understand and flexible product configuration capabilities is essential in the cloud product ordering process. This is because cloud products typically come with complex technical parameters, and users need to configure them based on their specific scenarios and requirements during the ordering process.

The correct configuration of these parameters determines whether users can successfully use the cloud product and integrate it effectively with their existing technology platforms. Additionally, it also affects whether users can adopt the most cost-effective product configuration scheme.

Therefore, offering user-friendly and flexible product configuration capabilities is essential for a successful cloud business.

1. **Simplified Interface:** Design an intuitive and user-friendly interface that guides users through the ordering process step by step. Use clear language, simple layouts, and visual aids to help users understand their options and make informed decisions.

2. **Wizard-Based Approach:** Implement a wizard-based approach that breaks down the ordering process into smaller, manageable steps. Each step should focus on a specific aspect of the configuration, such as selecting resources, specifying settings, and reviewing the order before finalizing.

3. **Guided Configuration:** Offer guided configuration options that help users choose the most suitable settings based on their requirements. Provide recommendations, best practices, and tooltips to explain each configuration option and its implications.

4. **Predefined Templates:** Provide predefined templates or configuration presets for common use cases or scenarios. These templates can serve as starting points for users, allowing them to quickly configure their cloud products without needing to start from scratch.

5. **Interactive Tools:** Incorporate interactive tools such as sliders, dropdown menus, and toggle switches to facilitate configuration adjustments in real-time. Enable users to preview changes instantly and see how different configurations impact performance, cost, and other factors.

6. **Progress Indicators:** Display progress indicators or breadcrumbs to show users where they are in the ordering

process and how many steps are remaining. This helps users understand the overall workflow and encourages them to complete the process.

7. **Contextual Help:** Offer contextual help resources, such as inline help text, tooltips, and links to documentation, to provide additional information and guidance throughout the ordering process. Address common questions, concerns, and misconceptions to enhance user confidence and clarity.

4.1.1 Configuration vs Scenario

Clear association between the configuration of cloud products and their respective scenarios is very helpful for cloud users.

By understanding how different configurations align with specific usage scenarios, users can:

- Select configurations tailored to their specific workload requirements, ensuring optimal performance and efficiency.

- Choose configurations that match their usage patterns, avoiding over-provisioning and unnecessary costs.

Offer examples and case studies related to various usage scenarios, helping users understand how to configure based on their business needs. These examples may include best practices, success stories, and real-world application scenarios.

4.1.2 Availability Check

Before placing an order, it's crucial to verify that the required resources, such as virtual machines, storage, and network bandwidth, are available from the cloud service provider. This ensures that the necessary infrastructure components are ready to support the deployment of the purchased applications and services.

Resource capacity management for cloud products involves the efficient allocation and utilization of various resources such as computing power, storage, and network bandwidth to meet the dynamic demands of customers while ensuring optimal performance, scalability, and cost-effectiveness.

Based on resource usage data and growth projections, capacity planning involves estimating future resource demands and ensuring that sufficient capacity is available to meet these demands. It includes forecasting resource needs, scaling infrastructure, and provisioning additional resources as needed.

By integrating availability checks with resource capacity management, cloud providers can ensure that their services remain highly available, resilient, and capable of handling varying workload demands. This holistic approach helps maintain service quality, customer satisfaction, and competitive advantage in the cloud market.

Designing a capacity check, reservation, and deduction system for cloud products that optimizes resource utilization, ensures efficient allocation, and provides a seamless experience for customers:

1. **Resource Monitoring**: Implement a system to continuously monitor the capacity and utilization of cloud resources, such as virtual machines, storage, and networking components.

2. **Reservation System**: Develop a reservation system that allows customers to reserve resources in advance based on their anticipated usage requirements. This system should consider factors such as resource type, quantity, duration, and availability.

   Ensure real-time synchronization between the reservation system and ordering system to reflect the latest availability status and reservation updates. Any changes made in either system should be immediately reflected in the other to maintain data consistency.

3. **Capacity Check**: When customers request resources, perform a real-time capacity check to ensure that sufficient resources are available to fulfill their request. This check should take into account the current utilization levels and any existing reservations.

4. **Automatic Reservation**: If the requested resources are available, automatically reserve them for the customer's use within the specified timeframe. Update the reservation system to reflect the allocated resources and adjust the available capacity accordingly.

   Establish clear associations between orders and reservations to track resource allocation accurately. Each order should be linked to the corresponding reservations, allowing for easy reference and management.

   Allow customers to modify their orders and associated reservations as needed. Enable them to adjust reservation parameters such as quantity, duration, or resource types even after order placement, ensuring flexibility and adaptability.

5. **Resource Deduction**: Deduct the reserved resources from the available capacity pool to prevent overcommitment and ensure accurate resource allocation. Update the resource utilization metrics accordingly.

6. **Expiry and Release**: Implement mechanisms to manage reservation expiry and resource release. Automatically release reserved resources when the reservation period expires or when the customer cancels the reservation.

Implement seamless handling of order cancellations and reservation releases. When customers cancel orders, automatically release the reserved resources back into the available pool for other customers to utilize.

7. **Alerts and Notifications**: Set up alerts and notifications to inform customers and administrators of reservation status changes, such as successful reservations, impending expiry, or resource depletion.

By integrating the reservation system with the ordering system, CSPs can streamline the process of resource allocation, enhance customer satisfaction, and improve overall operational efficiency.

4.1.3 Pricing Display

Displaying pricing information for cloud product configuration is essential for transparency and helping customers make informed decisions.

CSPs should Clearly display the features and capabilities associated with each pricing tier or configuration option. Ensure that customers understand the trade-offs between different features and their corresponding costs.

Meanwhile, CPSs should make pricing information easily accessible and prominently displayed throughout the product configuration process. This includes displaying pricing details on product pages, configuration screens, and checkout pages.

Clearly specify the currency used for pricing and the billing period (e.g., monthly, annually) to avoid confusion.

Clearly communicate any additional costs such as setup fees, data transfer fees, or usage overages. Similarly, highlight any discounts or promotions that may apply to the selected configuration.

For customers to compare the total prices of different product configurations, CSP need to implement tools or calculators that allow customers to dynamically estimate the cost of their selected configuration in real-time. This helps users understand the financial implications of their choices before making a commitment.

For the same product configuration, CSPs should be able to provide the total price under different pricing models, allowing customers to choose the pricing model that suits their needs.

To design a structured and clear pricing display for cloud product ordering, consider the following points:

- **Simple Layout**: Keep the layout clean and intuitive, with clear sections for each component of the pricing.

- **Transparent Pricing**: Provide detailed breakdowns of costs, including base prices, additional features, usage-based charges, and any applicable taxes or fees.

- **Comparison Tools**: Include features that allow customers to compare pricing options easily, such as side-by-side comparisons or interactive calculators.

- **Visual Representation**: Utilize charts, graphs, or visual aids to illustrate pricing structures and help customers understand complex pricing models more easily.

- **Mobile Compatibility**: Ensure that the pricing display is optimized for mobile devices, allowing customers to view and interact with it seamlessly on smartphones and tablets.

- **Help Resources**: Provide explanatory tooltips, FAQs, or links to support resources to assist customers in understanding pricing terms and options.

- **Clear Call-to-Action**: Include prominent buttons or prompts for customers to proceed with their selected configuration or to contact sales for further assistance.

- **Accessible Language**: Use clear and concise language that is easy for customers to understand, avoiding technical jargon or industry-specific terms whenever possible.

- **Feedback Mechanism**: Allow customers to provide feedback on the pricing display to help identify areas for improvement and ensure ongoing optimization.

4.1.4 Product Recommendations

Utilize smart algorithms and machine learning techniques to recommend the most suitable configuration options based on user-provided information and scenario characteristics. This can be achieved by analyzing user behavior, patterns, and historical data.

AI-powered NLP interfaces can simplify the process of configuring cloud products by allowing users to describe their requirements in natural language. These interfaces can interpret user input, suggest appropriate configurations, and automate the provisioning process, making it easier and more intuitive for users to optimize their cloud setups.

Virtual assistants and chatbots equipped with AI capabilities can help customers with product selection and configuration by answering questions, providing product information, and guiding users through the selection process based on their preferences and requirements.

Offer professional consulting services and technical support to assist users in customizing configurations based on their usage scenarios. This may include pre-sales consultations, real-time support, and customized solution design services.

AI-driven dynamic optimization techniques can continuously adjust cloud configurations in real-time based on changing workload demands, resource availability, and cost considerations. This ensures that cloud resources are always aligned with current requirements, maximizing efficiency and cost-effectiveness.

AI-powered predictive analytics can forecast future resource demands and workload patterns, enabling proactive adjustment of cloud configurations to accommodate anticipated changes. This helps in optimizing resource allocation, minimizing over-provisioning, and avoiding performance bottlenecks.

These AI-driven tools for product selection and configuration aim to enhance the customer experience, streamline the purchasing process, and increase sales by providing personalized recommendations and seamless customization options based on individual preferences and requirements.

4.2 Shopping Cart

The shopping cart plays an important role in the ordering process for cloud products.

Instead of placing individual orders for each cloud product separately, the shopping cart enables customers to consolidate their selections into a single order, which allows them to aggregate these selections in one place before proceeding to checkout, providing a convenient overview of their chosen items. This simplifies the ordering process and reduces the complexity of managing multiple transactions.

By displaying all selected items in the shopping cart, customers gain visibility and transparency into their order contents, including product details, quantities, and prices. This transparency helps customers review their selections before finalizing the order.

The shopping cart serves as a temporary storage space for customer orders until they are ready to be finalized. This allows customers to review, modify, or save their orders for future reference before completing the checkout process.

Once customers are satisfied with their selections, the shopping cart seamlessly transitions them to the checkout process, where they can provide payment and shipping information to complete the order. This streamlined checkout experience enhances convenience and reduces friction in the ordering process.

From CSPs perspective, they can leverage the shopping cart to implement cross-selling and upselling strategies by recommending complementary or upgraded products based on the customer's selections. This can help increase average order value and enhance customer satisfaction.

Overall, the shopping cart enhances the ordering experience for cloud products by providing a centralized platform for product aggregation, customization, cost estimation, and order management, ultimately leading to improved customer satisfaction and higher conversion rates.

4.2.1 Good shopping cart

Designing a good shopping cart function for cloud products involves considering several key elements to ensure a seamless and user-friendly experience. Here are some points to design an effective shopping cart function:

1. **Intuitive Interface**: Design a clean and intuitive interface that clearly displays the selected cloud products, quantities, prices, and any relevant details. Use familiar cart icons and layout conventions to make it easy for users to understand and navigate.

2. **Quantity Adjustment**: Allow users to easily adjust the quantity of each cloud product in their cart. Provide intuitive controls, such as +/- buttons or dropdown menus, for users to increase or decrease quantities as needed.

3. **Product Removal**: Enable users to remove individual cloud products from their cart if they no longer wish to purchase them. Include a prominent "Remove" or "Delete" option next to each product for quick and easy removal.

4. **Price Summary**: Display a summary of the total cost of the selected cloud products, including any applicable taxes, fees, or discounts. Update the price summary in real-time as users make changes to their cart to provide accurate cost estimates.

5. **Promotional Messages**: Utilize the shopping cart to communicate any promotional messages, discounts, or special offers relevant to the user's selections. Highlight savings or incentives to encourage users to proceed to checkout.

6. **Save for Later**: Offer users the option to save selected cloud products for later if they are not ready to purchase them immediately. Include a "Save for Later" or "Wishlist" feature that allows users to revisit and easily move items back to their cart when desired.

7. **Checkout Button**: Provide a prominent and easily accessible "Checkout" button that directs users to the checkout process when they are ready to complete their purchase. Ensure the button is clearly labeled and stands out visually to encourage conversion.

8. **Error Handling**: Anticipate and address potential errors or issues that users may encounter, such as out-of-stock items or invalid configurations. Provide clear error messages and

guidance on how to resolve the issues to minimize frustration and confusion.

4.2.2 Compatibility Check

For cloud products, the shopping cart function should provide a capability different from that of other industries: checking and verifying the compatibility between the products placed in the cart. This includes both functional compatibility and quantity matching.

- **Functional Compatibility Check**: The shopping cart should be able to detect the functional compatibility between the selected cloud products. This means the system needs to verify whether the selected products can work together seamlessly in the same environment and whether they have mutually compatible features and characteristics. For example, if a user selects a database service and a storage service, the cart should check if they can integrate seamlessly and meet the user's needs.

- **Quantity Matching Check**: The shopping cart should also ensure that the quantity and configuration of the selected products match. This includes checking whether the quotas, capacities, throughput, etc., of cloud resources are sufficient to meet the user's needs. If a user selects a service that requires a large amount of resources, the cart should remind the user to adjust the quantity or configuration of other related products to ensure overall compatibility.

To achieve these functions, the shopping cart system may need to integrate with the configuration management system or resource scheduling system of cloud products to obtain detailed information about product functionalities and quantities, and perform the necessary checks and verifications accordingly.

Additionally, the shopping cart interface should provide clear feedback and guidance to help users understand and address any potential compatibility or quantity matching issues. This ensures that users can accurately obtain product combinations during the shopping process and meet their needs to the greatest extent possible.

4.3 Order Payment

A user-friendly payment experience helps reduce cart abandonment rates. Complicated or confusing payment processes can frustrate customers and lead them to abandon their orders midway. By streamlining the payment process, CSPs can minimize abandonment rates and increase conversion rates.

A secure and reliable payment experience builds trust and credibility with customers. Providing secure payment options and protecting sensitive financial information instills confidence in customers, encouraging them to transact with the CSP.

Ensuring compliance with payment industry regulations and implementing robust security measures is crucial for protecting customer data and maintaining trust. A reliable payment experience includes features such as PCI compliance, encryption, and fraud detection to safeguard sensitive information.

A smooth and hassle-free payment experience enhances customer satisfaction. Customers appreciate a seamless checkout process without technical glitches or delays, leading to a positive overall impression of the CSP's services.

Overall, a positive payment experience enhances customer satisfaction, builds trust, reduces friction in the purchasing process, and contributes to the CSP's success in a competitive marketplace.

Designing a good payment function for cloud product ordering involves creating a seamless and secure checkout process that enhances user experience and encourages conversions. Here are some key steps to design an effective payment function:

1. **Offer Multiple Payment Methods**: Provide customers with a variety of payment options, including credit/debit cards, digital wallets (e.g., PayPal, Apple Pay, Google Pay), bank transfers, and other popular payment methods. Catering to diverse preferences increases convenience and flexibility for customers.

2. **Streamline Checkout Process**: Simplify the checkout process to minimize steps and reduce friction. Use a single-page or multi-step checkout interface with clear progress indicators to guide customers through each stage. Enable guest checkout to allow users to complete purchases without creating an account, although account creation should be encouraged for future convenience.

3. **Clear Pricing and Transparency**: Display pricing information, including any applicable taxes, fees, and discounts, prominently throughout the checkout process. Provide customers with a summary of their order before payment confirmation, allowing them to review and modify their selections if necessary.

4. **Mobile Optimization**: Ensure that the payment function is optimized for mobile devices, as an increasing number of customers use smartphones and tablets for online shopping. The payment interface should be responsive, easy to navigate, and compatible with various screen sizes and orientations.

5. **Security Measures**: Implement robust security measures to protect customer payment information and prevent

unauthorized access. Use SSL encryption to secure data transmission, comply with PCI DSS standards, and integrate fraud detection mechanisms to identify and mitigate suspicious transactions.

6. **Error Handling and Support**: Provide clear error messages and guidance to users in case of payment failures or issues. Offer customer support channels, such as live chat, email, or phone support, to assist users with payment-related inquiries or problems.

7. **Confirmation and Receipts**: Display a confirmation page or message after successful payment processing, reassuring customers that their order has been successfully placed. Send email receipts or order confirmation messages with detailed purchase information for customers' records.

4.3.1 Payment Method

A payment method refers to the means by which a customer provides funds to complete a financial transaction. It can include various forms of payment instruments or channels used to transfer money from the customer to the seller or service provider.

For cloud service providers (CSPs), providing suitable payment methods for different countries and regions is crucial due to their global or multi-country/region business coverage. Different countries and regions have different payment habits, regulations, and currencies, so offering diverse payment options can better meet the needs of global customers and increase purchase conversion rates. Here are some payment method suggestions for the global market:

1. **Credit/debit cards:** Accept major international credit cards and debit cards such as Visa, Mastercard, and American

Express. This is one of the most common payment methods worldwide.

2. **Digital wallets:** Integrate popular digital wallet services such as PayPal, Apple Pay, Google Pay, etc., to facilitate transactions for customers who prefer using these platforms.

3. **Bank transfers:** Provide options for bank transfers or direct debits from customers' bank accounts, offering customers more flexible payment methods suitable for different countries and regions.

4. **Virtual bank cards:** Allow customers to use virtual bank cards or prepaid cards for payment, which is popular in some countries and regions, especially for customers concerned about online security.

5. **Cryptocurrency:** Consider accepting cryptocurrency payments such as Bitcoin, Ethereum, etc., suitable for customers who want to protect personal privacy and enjoy the benefits of digital currencies.

6. **Multi-currency payments:** Support multiple currency payments to meet the different needs of customers and reduce the inconvenience of currency conversion.

Comply with payment regulations and compliance requirements in various countries and regions to ensure the legality and security of the payment process, enhancing customer trust.

Each payment method has its own advantages, limitations, and security considerations, and businesses often offer multiple payment options to accommodate the preferences and needs of their customers. Choosing the right mix of payment methods can help optimize the checkout experience, increase conversion rates, and meet the diverse needs of customers.

Due to the majority of cloud service products being post-paid, CSPs need to carefully consider the compatibility of payment methods and billing cycles to prevent bad debts or malicious arrears.

For example, cloud products billed on an hourly basis often require customers to provide credit card payments. This allows CSPs to automatically process payments in real-time from the credit card. Additionally, in cases where customers are unable to complete payments, CSPs can take prompt actions such as notifications and service suspensions to prevent the accumulation of large unpaid bills. This approach not only safeguards the interests of the CSP but also mitigates the occurrence of bill shock for customers.

4.3.2 Payment Security

During the payment process, several risks can occur, posing potential threats to both the customer and the cloud service provider (CSP). Some common risks include:

1. **Fraudulent Transactions**: Hackers or cybercriminals may attempt to make unauthorized transactions using stolen payment credentials or by exploiting vulnerabilities in the payment system.

2. **Data Breaches**: Payment information, such as credit card numbers or bank account details, may be intercepted or compromised during transmission, leading to data breaches and potential financial losses for customers and CSPs.

3. **Identity Theft**: Cybercriminals may use stolen personal information to impersonate customers and make fraudulent purchases, leading to identity theft and financial fraud.

4. **Payment Processing Errors**: Technical glitches or system malfunctions in the payment processing infrastructure can

result in errors such as overcharging, double billing, or failed transactions, leading to customer dissatisfaction and loss of revenue for CSPs.

5. **Payment Gateway Vulnerabilities**: Weaknesses or vulnerabilities in the payment gateway infrastructure can be exploited by attackers to gain unauthorized access, manipulate transactions, or steal sensitive payment data.

6. **Regulatory Compliance Violations**: Non-compliance with regulatory requirements, such as the Payment Card Industry Data Security Standard (PCI DSS) or General Data Protection Regulation (GDPR), can result in penalties, fines, and reputational damage for CSPs.

7. **Insufficient Funds**: Customers may attempt to make payments without sufficient funds in their accounts, leading to failed transactions and potential disputes.

8. **Phishing and Social Engineering**: Cybercriminals may use phishing emails, fake websites, or social engineering tactics to trick customers into divulging their payment information, leading to fraudulent transactions or identity theft.

9. **Third-Party Risks**: Risks associated with third-party payment processors, vendors, or service providers, such as data breaches, service disruptions, or compliance failures, can impact the security and reliability of the payment process.

To mitigate these risks, CSPs should implement robust security measures, such as encryption, multi-factor authentication, fraud detection systems, and regular security audits, to protect payment transactions and customer data. Additionally, educating customers about safe payment practices and providing secure payment options can help prevent fraud and enhance trust in the payment process.

4.3.3 Anti Money Laundering

Cloud product ordering can be attractive for money laundering due to several factors:

1. **Anonymity**: Cloud product ordering can be conducted online, allowing individuals to remain relatively anonymous. Criminals may exploit this anonymity to conduct illicit transactions without revealing their true identities.

2. **Global Reach**: Cloud services are often available globally, allowing individuals to access them from anywhere in the world. This global reach makes it easier for criminals to conduct cross-border transactions and move funds internationally to obfuscate their origin and destination.

3. **Complexity**: Cloud product ordering can involve complex transactions and payment methods, making it difficult for authorities to trace the flow of funds and identify suspicious activities. Criminals may exploit this complexity to conceal their illicit transactions within legitimate business activities.

4. **Large Volumes of Data**: Cloud services often involve the storage and processing of large volumes of data. Criminals may use cloud services to store and transfer large amounts of illicit data or to conduct illegal activities such as cybercrime, fraud, or intellectual property theft.

5. **Automation and Scalability**: Cloud services offer automation and scalability features that allow users to quickly scale up or down their usage based on demand. Criminals

may exploit this scalability to conduct large-scale money laundering operations without attracting suspicion.

The combination of anonymity, global reach, and complexity makes cloud product ordering an attractive avenue for money laundering activities. It is essential for cloud service providers to implement robust anti-money laundering measures to detect and prevent illicit activities on their platforms.

To combat money laundering during cloud product ordering, cloud service providers (CSPs) can implement several anti-money laundering (AML) measures:

1. **Customer Due Diligence (CDD)**: Implement robust CDD procedures to verify the identity of customers before allowing them to order cloud products. This may involve collecting identification documents, verifying business registration details, and conducting enhanced due diligence for high-risk customers.

2. **Transaction Monitoring**: Implement automated transaction monitoring systems to detect suspicious patterns or unusual activities in cloud product orders. This may include monitoring for large transactions, multiple transactions below reporting thresholds, or transactions involving high-risk jurisdictions. AI-powered transaction monitoring systems can continuously monitor financial transactions in real-time, flagging potentially suspicious activities for further review. By automating this process, AI can reduce false positives and improve the efficiency of AML compliance operations.

3. **Know Your Customer (KYC) Compliance**: Ensure compliance with KYC regulations by collecting relevant information about customers, such as their identity, business activities, and source of funds. Conduct ongoing monitoring

of customer accounts to detect any changes in behavior or risk profile.

4. **Enhanced Due Diligence (EDD)**: Conduct enhanced due diligence on high-risk customers or transactions, such as those involving politically exposed persons (PEPs), high-value transactions, or customers from high-risk jurisdictions. This may involve conducting additional background checks, obtaining additional documentation, or seeking approval from senior management.

5. **Sanctions Screening**: Screen customers against international sanctions lists and watchlists to ensure compliance with sanctions regulations. Implement automated screening systems to flag any matches and escalate them for further investigation.

6. **Reporting Obligations**: Establish procedures for reporting suspicious activities to the relevant authorities, such as financial intelligence units or law enforcement agencies. Ensure that employees understand their reporting obligations and have access to channels for reporting suspicious activities internally.

7. **Risk-Based Approach**: Implement a risk-based approach to AML compliance, where resources and controls are proportionate to the level of risk posed by customers, transactions, and jurisdictions. This may involve conducting risk assessments and adjusting AML measures accordingly.

AI can significantly enhance anti-money laundering (AML) efforts by leveraging advanced algorithms and machine learning techniques to analyze large volumes of data, detect patterns, and identify suspicious activities more effectively.

AI can analyze vast amounts of transactional data, customer information, and other relevant data sources to identify unusual patterns or anomalies indicative of potential money laundering activities. AI algorithms can process structured and unstructured data from various sources, including financial transactions, emails, social media, and more.

AI models can be trained to recognize patterns associated with known money laundering techniques, such as structuring transactions, layering funds, and smurfing. By identifying these patterns, AI systems can flag potentially suspicious activities for further investigation.

4.4 Provisioning and Deployment

Efficient provisioning and deployment processes enable customers to quickly access and start using the cloud products they have ordered. This agility is particularly important in fast-paced business environments where time-to-market is critical.

Automated provisioning and deployment workflows streamline the process and reduce the potential for errors. Orchestration tools can automate complex deployment scenarios, ensuring consistency and reliability across deployments.

The functional framework for cloud product provisioning encompasses a set of processes and capabilities designed to efficiently and effectively provision resources and deploy services in a cloud environment.

1. **Resource Allocation**: This involves the allocation of resources such as computing instances, storage volumes, and network resources based on customer requirements. It includes capacity planning to ensure that sufficient resources are available to meet demand.

2. **Service Configuration**: Service configuration involves setting up and configuring the software and infrastructure components required to deliver the desired cloud services. This may include installing operating systems, middleware, and application software, as well as configuring network settings and security policies.

3. **Automation and Orchestration**: Automation and orchestration tools are used to automate provisioning tasks and orchestrate the deployment of complex cloud environments. This helps streamline the provisioning process, reduce manual errors, and improve efficiency.

4. **Template Management**: Template management involves the creation, storage, and management of templates or blueprints that define standardized configurations for provisioning cloud resources. Templates can include predefined configurations for virtual machines, containers, network settings, and application deployments.

5. **Resource Tracking and Management**: Resource tracking and management capabilities enable organizations to monitor and manage provisioned resources throughout their lifecycle. This includes tracking resource utilization, managing access permissions, and decommissioning resources when they are no longer needed.

6. **Integration with Identity and Access Management (IAM)**: Integration with IAM systems enables organizations to control access to provisioned resources based on user roles, permissions, and policies. This helps enforce security and compliance requirements and ensures that only authorized users can access cloud services.

7. **Monitoring and Reporting**: Monitoring and reporting functionalities provide visibility into the status, performance, and usage of provisioned resources. This includes real-time monitoring of resource health and performance metrics, as well as generating reports on resource utilization and costs.

4.4.1 Provisioning Orchestration

Provisioning orchestration is crucial for cloud orders because it streamlines and automates the process of deploying resources and services in a cloud environment.

Provisioning orchestration automates repetitive and manual tasks involved in provisioning cloud resources, such as deploying virtual machines, configuring networks, and installing software. This improves operational efficiency by reducing the time and effort required to fulfill orders.

Cloud environments often consist of multiple interconnected components and services. Orchestration simplifies the management of this complexity by coordinating the provisioning of all required resources and ensuring that they are properly configured and integrated.

There are several tools available in the market that facilitate cloud product provisioning orchestration. These tools offer various features and capabilities to automate and streamline the deployment of cloud resources and services. Some popular examples include:

1. **Terraform**: Terraform, developed by HashiCorp, is an open-source infrastructure as code (IaC) tool that allows users to define and provision cloud infrastructure using declarative configuration files. It supports multiple cloud providers, including AWS, Azure, Google Cloud Platform (GCP), and

more, enabling users to manage infrastructure as code and automate provisioning workflows.

2. **AWS CloudFormation**: AWS CloudFormation is a service provided by Amazon Web Services (AWS) that allows users to define and provision AWS infrastructure resources using templates. It enables users to create and manage a collection of related AWS resources as a single unit, automating the provisioning and deployment process.

3. **Azure Resource Manager (ARM) Templates**: Azure Resource Manager (ARM) Templates are JSON files used to define and provision Azure resources in Microsoft Azure. Similar to AWS CloudFormation, ARM Templates enable users to automate the deployment of Azure infrastructure resources and manage them as a single unit.

4. **Google Cloud Deployment Manager**: Google Cloud Deployment Manager is a service provided by Google Cloud Platform (GCP) that allows users to define and deploy Google Cloud Platform resources using configuration files written in YAML or Python. It provides a declarative approach to infrastructure management, enabling users to automate the deployment and provisioning of GCP resources.

5. **Ansible**: Ansible is an open-source automation tool that can be used for provisioning and configuring cloud infrastructure, as well as managing IT environments. It uses YAML-based playbooks to define provisioning tasks and can be integrated with various cloud providers to automate infrastructure deployment and management.

These are just a few examples of tools available for cloud product provisioning orchestration. Depending on the specific requirements and preferences of an organization, different tools may be more suitable for automating and managing their cloud infrastructure provisioning workflows.

4.4.2 Activating AI Product

Activating an AI product may involve some specialized considerations compared to traditional software products due to the unique nature of AI technology. Here are some specialties to consider when activating an AI product:

1. **Data Preparation and Integration**: AI models require high-quality data for training, validation, and inference. Activating an AI product often involves preparing and integrating datasets from various sources, ensuring data quality, and performing preprocessing tasks such as cleaning, normalization, and feature engineering.

2. **Model Training and Tuning**: For AI products that include machine learning models, activation may involve training and fine-tuning these models using the prepared data. This process often requires expertise in machine learning algorithms, model selection, hyperparameter tuning, and optimization techniques to achieve the desired performance metrics.

3. **Deployment Architecture**: Activating an AI product involves deploying the trained models into production environments where they can make predictions or generate insights in real-time. This requires designing and implementing scalable, reliable, and efficient deployment architectures, such as containerized deployments using platforms like Docker or Kubernetes.

4. **Integration with Existing Systems**: AI products often need to integrate with existing systems and workflows

within an organization. Activation may involve integrating AI capabilities into existing software applications, business processes, or data pipelines, ensuring seamless interoperability and data flow between different components.

5. **Monitoring and Maintenance**: Once activated, AI products require ongoing monitoring and maintenance to ensure optimal performance, reliability, and security. This may involve setting up monitoring systems to track model performance metrics, detecting drift or degradation, and implementing strategies for model retraining or updates.

6. **Ethical and Regulatory Considerations**: Activating an AI product requires consideration of ethical and regulatory implications related to data privacy, bias, fairness, transparency, and compliance with industry standards and regulations. This may involve implementing measures to mitigate bias, ensure transparency in AI decision-making, and comply with data protection regulations such as GDPR or HIPAA.

Overall, activating an AI product requires a multidisciplinary approach, involving expertise in data science, machine learning, software engineering, deployment infrastructure, and domain-specific knowledge to ensure successful deployment and operation in real-world environments.

4.5 Subscription Management

Subscription management for cloud products involves the processes and tools used to manage the subscription lifecycle of customers who have purchased or subscribed to cloud services. This includes activities related to subscription creation, modification, renewal, and cancellation, as well as customer communication throughout the subscription period. Key aspects of subscription management for cloud products include:

- **Subscription Modification**: Allowing customers to modify their subscriptions as needed, such as upgrading or downgrading service plans, adding or removing features, or adjusting billing cycles. This requires flexibility in the subscription management system to accommodate changes without disrupting service.

- **Subscription Renewal**: Managing the renewal process to ensure that subscriptions are automatically renewed at the end of the billing period, unless explicitly cancelled by the customer. This may involve sending renewal reminders, updating payment information, and adjusting subscription terms as necessary.

- **Subscription Cancellation:** Subscription cancellation refers to the process of terminating a customer's subscription to a service or product. In the context of cloud products, subscription cancellation involves ending the recurring billing and usage of cloud services by a customer.

- **Customer Communication**: Providing proactive communication with customers regarding their subscriptions, such as billing notifications, renewal reminders, service updates, and promotional offers. Effective communication helps to build trust and loyalty with customers and reduces the likelihood of churn.

4.5.1 Subscription Modification

Subscription modification for cloud products involves allowing users to make changes to their existing subscription plans. This could include upgrading or downgrading service tiers, adding or removing features, adjusting billing cycles, or making any other modifications to better suit the user's evolving needs. This flexibility allows users to adapt their subscriptions as their requirements change over time, providing them with a more customized and satisfactory experience.

Adjusting subscription plans may involve changes in billing cycles, pricing structures, and payment methods. Ensuring accurate billing and pricing adjustments while minimizing errors can be a challenge, especially when dealing with prorated charges or refunds.

Subscription modifications may require technical integration with billing systems, customer management platforms, and other backend systems. Ensuring seamless integration and coordination between different systems can be complex, especially in multi-cloud or hybrid cloud environments.

Providing a seamless and intuitive user experience for subscription modification is essential. Users should be able to easily understand their options, make changes efficiently, and receive confirmation of their modifications promptly. Designing user-friendly interfaces and workflows while accommodating diverse user preferences can be challenging.

Implementing a subscription change for a cloud product involves several steps to ensure a smooth and seamless transition for both the customer and the service provider. Here's a general outline of the implementation process:

1. **Evaluate Customer Request**: Start by assessing the customer's request for a subscription change. Determine the specific changes requested, such as upgrading or downgrading the subscription plan, changing billing cycles, adding or removing features, etc.

2. **Check Eligibility**: Verify if the customer is eligible for the requested subscription change based on factors such as current subscription status, contractual obligations, payment history, etc.

3. **Calculate Pricing**: Determine the pricing implications of the subscription change, including any prorated charges or refunds, adjustments to recurring billing amounts, and updates to payment schedules.

4. **Update Billing System**: Make the necessary updates to the billing system to reflect the changes in the customer's subscription. This may involve modifying billing cycles, updating pricing tiers, adjusting invoice generation settings, etc.

5. **Adjust Service Configuration**: If the subscription change involves modifying the provisioned services or features, update the service configuration accordingly. This may require provisioning or deprovisioning resources, activating or deactivating features, adjusting access controls, etc.

6. **Communicate with Customer**: Inform the customer about the status of their subscription change request, including confirmation of the requested changes, details of pricing adjustments, and any other relevant information. Provide clear and timely communication to keep the customer informed throughout the process.

7. **Verify Changes**: Double-check the implemented changes to ensure accuracy and completeness. Verify that the customer's subscription has been updated correctly in the billing system and that the associated services reflect the requested modifications.

By following these steps and maintaining clear communication with the customer throughout the process, you can effectively implement subscription changes for cloud products while minimizing disruptions and ensuring a positive customer experience.

4.5.2 Subscription Renewal

Subscription renewal for cloud products refers to the process of extending a customer's existing subscription for a specified term, typically after the initial subscription period expires.

Subscription renewal ensures that customers maintain uninterrupted access to the cloud services they rely on for their business operations. Without renewal, access to essential resources, applications, and data stored in the cloud could be disrupted, impacting productivity and workflows.

Non-renewal or lapses in subscription can lead to service suspension or termination by the cloud service provider. This could result in temporary or prolonged downtime for the customer's applications and systems, disrupting business operations and potentially causing financial losses.

At the same time, subscription renewals contribute to a steady and predictable stream of revenue for cloud service providers (CSPs). By retaining existing customers and renewing their subscriptions, CSPs can maintain a stable financial foundation and forecast revenue more accurately.

Implementing a good subscription renewal mechanism for cloud products involves several key steps and considerations to ensure seamless and efficient renewal processes:

- **Clear Communication**: Provide clear and timely communication to customers about upcoming subscription renewals. Notify them well in advance before the renewal date, outlining the renewal process, any changes in pricing or terms, and instructions on how to proceed.

- **Automated Renewal Options**: Offer automated renewal options to streamline the process for customers who wish to continue their subscriptions without manual intervention. Allow customers to opt-in for auto-renewal during the initial subscription setup or through their account settings.

- **Flexible Renewal Terms**: Provide flexibility in renewal terms to accommodate varying customer preferences and business needs. Offer options for monthly, annual, or multi-year subscription renewals, allowing customers to choose the most suitable term for their budget and requirements.

- **Proactive Customer Engagement**: Proactively engage with customers nearing their renewal dates to remind them of upcoming renewals and encourage timely action. Use email notifications, in-app messages, or personalized alerts to prompt customers to renew their subscriptions.

- **Streamlined Renewal Process**: Simplify the renewal process as much as possible to minimize friction for customers. Offer one-click or single-step renewal options directly from the customer's account dashboard or through a dedicated renewal portal, eliminating unnecessary steps or paperwork.

- **Incentives and Discounts**: Encourage subscription renewals by offering incentives, discounts, or loyalty rewards to customers who renew their subscriptions promptly or commit to longer-term renewals. This can help incentivize renewals and increase customer retention rates.

- **Grace Periods and Reminders**: Provide a grace period after the renewal date to allow customers to renew their subscriptions without service interruption. Send reminders and notifications during the grace period to prompt customers to renew before their subscriptions expire.

- **Flexible Payment Options**: Offer flexible payment options for subscription renewals, including credit/debit card payments, bank transfers, invoicing, or alternative payment methods. Ensure that the payment process is secure, seamless, and compliant with relevant regulations.

- **Customer Support and Assistance**: Provide responsive customer support and assistance to address any questions, concerns, or issues related to subscription renewals. Offer multiple channels for customer support, including phone, email, live chat, or self-service resources.

By implementing these strategies, you can create a robust and customer-centric subscription renewal mechanism that enhances customer satisfaction, drives retention, and ensures the ongoing success of your cloud product offerings.

4.5.3 Subscription Cancellation

In many countries' consumer protection laws, it is typically mandated that businesses allow consumers to unsubscribe from services or products within a certain timeframe without providing a reason. And it is specified that in the case of prepaid product subscriptions, there must be a feature available for consumers to unsubscribe at any time, ensuring consumer autonomy and preventing businesses from coercively binding consumers.

Therefore, providing a good unsubscribe experience is crucial for CSPs to meet regulatory requirements and enhance brand image.

The unsubscribe or cancellation process typically begins when a customer submits a request to terminate their subscription. This request may be initiated through various channels, such as an online portal, email, phone call, or support ticket.

Upon receiving the cancellation request, the cloud provider may verify the identity of the customer and ensure that they have the authority to cancel the subscription. This step helps prevent unauthorized cancellations and ensures compliance with security and privacy policies.

The cloud provider acknowledges the cancellation request and confirms the details with the customer. This may involve providing information about the effective date of cancellation, any outstanding charges or obligations, and the consequences of cancellation (e.g., loss of access to services or data).

The provider adjusts the customer's billing account to reflect the cancellation of the subscription. Any prepaid fees or unused credits may be refunded to the customer, and future billing cycles are canceled or prorated accordingly.

At the scheduled cancellation date, the cloud services associated with the subscription are deactivated or terminated. This includes revoking access to the service platform, disabling user accounts, and removing any associated data or configurations.

Depending on the terms of the subscription agreement and applicable regulations, the provider may offer options for data retention or export prior to cancellation. Customers may be given the opportunity to download their data or transfer it to another service provider.

As part of the cancellation process, the provider may solicit feedback from the customer to understand the reasons for cancellation and identify areas for improvement. Customer feedback can inform future product development and customer retention strategies.

After the cancellation is complete, the provider may follow up with the customer to ensure that the process was completed satisfactorily and address any remaining questions or concerns. This helps maintain a positive customer experience even after cancellation.

Overall, effective subscription cancellation processes are essential for cloud providers to handle customer requests efficiently, maintain transparency and compliance, and preserve customer relationships even when they decide to discontinue their subscriptions.

5

BILLING

A billing platform for cloud products is a software system that facilitates the management and processing of billing and invoicing for cloud-based services. It serves as the backbone for monetizing cloud products and services, allowing providers to accurately track usage, calculate charges, generate invoices, and collect payments from customers.

The billing system is at the core of revenue generation for CSPs. It accurately calculates charges based on usage, subscription plans, and other factors, ensuring that customers are billed correctly for the services they consume.

Billing systems play a role in customer communication by sending out invoices, payment reminders, and other billing-related notifications. They provide customers with clear and timely information regarding their financial obligations and payment deadlines.

Effective billing communication is essential for maintaining a positive relationship between service providers and customers, fostering trust, transparency, and satisfaction in the billing process. It plays a crucial role in ensuring smooth, efficient, and mutually beneficial interactions between parties involved in financial transactions.

Automating the billing process streamlines operations for CSPs, reducing manual errors, administrative overhead, and billing cycle times. This efficiency allows CSPs to focus on delivering high-quality services and innovating their offerings.

The billing system plays a critical role in financial management by tracking revenue, receivables, and cash flow. It provides valuable insights into the financial health of the business and facilitates accurate financial reporting and forecasting.

Billing-related inquiries and issues are common among customers. An efficient billing system enables CSPs to handle customer inquiries promptly, resolve billing disputes effectively, and provide superior customer support.

Overall, a billing system is fundamental to the success of CSPs, enabling them to monetize their services, maintain financial health, ensure compliance, deliver excellent customer experiences, and drive business growth.

Typically, a billing system for cloud products consists of:

1. **Usage Data Collection:** The billing system collects usage data from various sources, such as cloud infrastructure, platforms, and applications. This data includes metrics related to resource utilization, storage, network traffic, and other service usage parameters.

2. **Metering and Rating:** Once usage data is collected, the billing system applies metering and rating processes to quantify the usage of cloud services. Metering involves measuring the quantity of consumed resources, while rating involves applying pricing rules and tariffs to calculate the cost of usage.

3. **Pricing and Billing Rules:** The billing system implements pricing models and billing rules that determine how usage is charged. This includes defining pricing tiers, discounts, promotions, and any applicable taxes or surcharges. Pricing

rules may vary based on factors such as service type, usage volume, and customer agreements.

4. **Invoice Generation:** The billing system generates invoices based on the metered usage and subscription details for each customer. Invoices typically include a breakdown of charges, usage summaries, billing periods, payment due dates, and other relevant information.

5. **Payment Processing:** Once invoices are generated, the billing system handles payment processing, including payment collection, reconciliation, and allocation. It supports various payment methods such as credit cards, bank transfers, electronic wallets, and automated clearing house (ACH) payments.

6. **Billing Notifications and Alerts:** The billing system sends notifications and alerts to customers regarding invoice generation, payment due dates, payment confirmations, and other billing-related events. These communications help ensure timely payments and enhance customer transparency.

7. **Revenue Recognition and Reporting:** The billing system facilitates revenue recognition by accurately recording and reporting revenue based on accounting standards such as ASC 606 or IFRS 15. It generates financial reports, dashboards, and analytics to provide insights into revenue performance, billing trends, and customer behavior.

8. **Compliance and Audit Trails:** To ensure compliance with regulatory requirements and industry standards, the billing system maintains audit trails, logs, and documentation of billing activities. It supports audit processes by providing transparency and traceability of billing transactions.

5.1 Usage Metering

Usage metering for cloud products and AI products involves the process of measuring and tracking the consumption of resources or services by customers. This is essential for accurately determining usage-based charges and providing transparent billing to customers.

1. **Cloud Products**:

   - Usage metering for cloud products involves tracking the usage of various resources and services provided by the cloud service provider (CSP), such as virtual machines, storage, databases, network bandwidth, and other infrastructure components.

   - Metering data is collected from the underlying cloud infrastructure, monitoring systems, or through APIs exposed by the cloud platform. This data includes metrics like CPU usage, memory usage, disk I/O, network traffic, and uptime.

   - Usage metering may be performed in real-time or periodically, depending on the billing and invoicing cycle agreed upon with the customer. Metered usage data is typically aggregated and stored for billing and reporting purposes.

2. **AI Products**:

   - Usage metering for AI products involves monitoring and quantifying the utilization of AI-related services, such as machine learning models, inference requests, training sessions, data processing, and API calls.

   - Metering data may include metrics related to the complexity of AI workloads, the volume of data processed, the duration of model inference, the number of predictions made, and other relevant parameters.

- Metering AI product usage requires instrumentation within the AI infrastructure, software libraries, or APIs to capture relevant usage metrics. This data is then aggregated and processed to generate usage reports and invoices for customers.

In both cases, usage metering plays a crucial role in enabling pay-as-you-go pricing models, where customers are billed based on their actual usage of resources or services. It provides transparency, accountability, and cost control for customers while allowing CSPs and AI service providers to monetize their offerings effectively. Additionally, usage metering data can inform capacity planning, resource optimization, and service-level agreements (SLAs) to enhance the overall customer experience.

5.1.1 Critical Role in Cloud Business

Usage metering not only the foundation of monetization of cloud business, but also plays a critical role in cloud business success:

- **Accuracy:** Usage metering ensures accurate billing by tracking and measuring the actual consumption of resources by customers. This includes quantifying usage of computing power, storage capacity, network bandwidth, and other resources used in the cloud environment.

- **Transparency:** Metering provides transparency in billing by giving customers visibility into their resource usage and associated costs. It enables customers to understand how their usage translates into charges, fostering trust and accountability in the billing process.

- **Cost Allocation:** Metering allows cloud providers to allocate costs accurately to individual customers or tenants based on their usage of resources. This enables fair and equitable distribution of costs among different users of the cloud platform.

- **Billing Flexibility:** Metering supports flexible billing models, such as pay-as-you-go, subscription-based, or usage-based pricing. Customers can choose the billing model that best aligns with their usage patterns and budgetary constraints, optimizing cost management and resource allocation.

- **Cost Optimization:** Usage data collected through metering can help customers optimize their resource usage and control costs. By analyzing usage patterns and identifying inefficiencies, customers can make informed decisions to right-size their infrastructure, optimize workflows, and minimize unnecessary spending.

- **Forecasting and Budgeting:** Metering data enables customers to forecast future usage and budget effectively for their cloud spending. By analyzing historical usage trends and projecting future requirements, customers can allocate resources and budget allocations more accurately, avoiding surprises and overspending.

- **Compliance and Auditing:** Metering provides an audit trail of resource usage and billing activities, supporting compliance with regulatory requirements and internal governance policies. It enables customers to track usage for compliance reporting, audit purposes, and internal accountability.

5.1.2 Typical Types of Cloud Metering

Different types of cloud products have different resource types and levels of virtualization, so the methods of collecting usage vary accordingly. Here are some common cloud products and their respective usage collection method:

1. **Virtual Machines (VMs):** For VM-based cloud products, usage is typically collected in metrics such as instance run time (instance hours), virtual CPU utilization, memory usage, and storage capacity.

   Monitoring agents can be installed on each VM instance to collect performance data and report it to the cloud provider.

2. **Containers:** For container-based cloud products, usage may include metrics such as container instance run time, CPU and memory utilization, number of containers, and network traffic.

   Container orchestration tools like Kubernetes can monitor and collect usage data for containers via APIs or plugins.

3. **Serverless Functions:** For serverless computing services, usage may be collected in metrics such as function invocation count, function execution time, memory usage, and network traffic.

   Monitoring and logging services provided by cloud providers can be used to record function invocations and executions.

4. **Storage Services:** For storage services, usage is typically collected in metrics such as storage capacity (storage volume), read/write operations, data transfer volume, and data retention time.

The storage services provided by cloud providers automatically record and report these metrics.

5. **Networking Services:** For networking services, usage may include metrics such as network bandwidth, traffic, and connection count.

   Network devices and firewalls can collect and report these metrics to monitor network traffic and connection activity.

6. **Database Services:** For database services, usage is typically collected in metrics such as database instance run time, query count, storage capacity, and data transfer volume.

   Database monitoring tools can monitor database performance and usage.

7. **Analytics and Artificial Intelligence (AI) Services:** For analytics and AI services, usage may include metrics such as data processing and analysis task execution time, model training and inference count, data transfer volume, and storage capacity.

   Analytics and AI platforms typically provide monitoring and reporting features to track these metrics.

8. **Internet of Things (IoT) Services:** For IoT services, usage may include metrics such as device connection count, message transfer volume, event processing count, and data storage volume.

   IoT platforms can collect and report these metrics to monitor devices and data flow.

In general, different types of cloud products require different usage collection methods to monitor and report resource usage. Cloud providers typically offer monitoring and management tools to help customers track and manage their cloud resource usage.

The mechanism for cloud usage metering involves the collection, aggregation, and processing of data related to the consumption of cloud resources by customers.

1. **Step1: Data Collection:** Cloud providers deploy monitoring agents or services across their infrastructure to collect data on resource usage. These agents gather information on various parameters such as CPU utilization, memory usage, storage capacity, network bandwidth, and application performance.

   Sometimes, monitoring agents or services may fail to collect usage data accurately due to technical issues, network disruptions, or misconfigurations. This can lead to discrepancies in reported usage and billing inaccuracies.

2. **Step2: Aggregation and Normalization:** The collected data is aggregated and normalized to ensure consistency and accuracy. This involves consolidating data from multiple sources, converting measurements into a standardized format, and aligning timestamps for accurate tracking.

   Aggregating and normalizing usage data from diverse sources and formats can be complex, particularly in hybrid or multi-cloud environments. Inconsistencies in data formats, timestamps, and measurement units may complicate the billing process.

3. **Step3: Granularity and Sampling:** Usage data may be collected at different levels of granularity, such as per-second, per-minute, or per-hour intervals. Sampling techniques may also be employed to capture usage patterns without

overwhelming the monitoring system with excessive data volume.

Determining the appropriate level of granularity for usage data collection can be challenging. Collecting data at too fine a granularity may result in excessive data volume and performance overhead, while collecting data at too coarse a granularity may lead to insufficient detail for accurate billing.

4. **Step4: Resource Identification:** Usage data is associated with specific cloud resources, such as virtual machines, containers, storage volumes, databases, and networking components. Each resource is uniquely identified to attribute usage accurately.

5.1.3 Typical Types of AI Product Metering

Metering for AI products involves tracking the usage of various AI-related services and resources. Here are some typical types of metering used for AI products:

1. **Model Inference Count**: Tracking the number of times a trained machine learning model is used to make predictions or classifications on new data.

2. **Training Duration**: Measuring the duration of time spent training machine learning models, including the time taken for data preprocessing, model training iterations, and evaluation.

3. **Data Processing Volume**: Monitoring the volume of data processed by AI pipelines, including data ingestion, transformation, feature extraction, and cleansing.

4. **API Calls**: Counting the number of calls made to AI-related APIs for tasks such as natural language processing (NLP),

image recognition, sentiment analysis, speech-to-text, and translation.

5. **Compute Resources Utilization**: Tracking the usage of computational resources (e.g., CPU, GPU, memory) during model training, inference, or data processing tasks.

6. **Storage Usage**: Measuring the amount of storage space occupied by AI-related data, including datasets, model checkpoints, training logs, and inference results.

7. **Custom Metrics**: Capturing custom performance metrics specific to AI applications, such as model accuracy, latency, throughput, error rates, and resource efficiency.

8. **Feature Usage**: Monitoring the usage of specific features or capabilities provided by AI platforms, libraries, or frameworks, such as autoML tools, pre-trained models, or specialized algorithms.

9. **Concurrency and Scalability**: Tracking the level of concurrency and scalability of AI workloads, including the number of parallel inference requests, simultaneous training sessions, or distributed processing tasks.

10. **SLA Compliance**: Evaluating the compliance of AI services with service-level agreements (SLAs) regarding performance, availability, reliability, and security.

By metering these aspects of AI product usage, providers can accurately bill customers, optimize resource allocation, track service quality, and improve overall operational efficiency. Additionally, usage metering data can inform pricing strategies, capacity planning, feature development, and customer support initiatives in the AI domain.

5.1.4 AI Powered Metering

AI (Artificial Intelligence) can help enhance cloud usage metering in several ways:

1. **Anomaly Detection:** AI-powered anomaly detection algorithms can analyze usage patterns and identify abnormal behavior, such as sudden spikes or drops in resource consumption. This helps detect potential issues or security threats that may impact billing accuracy.

2. **Predictive Analytics:** AI algorithms can analyze historical usage data to predict future resource demands. By forecasting usage trends and patterns, organizations can proactively adjust resource allocations and optimize costs.

3. **Optimization Recommendations:** AI-powered recommendation engines can analyze usage data and provide optimization suggestions to minimize costs. These recommendations may include rightsizing resources, identifying unused or underutilized resources, and suggesting cost-saving strategies.

Apart from the usage collection tools owned by major cloud providers, there are also some open-source usage collection tools in the industry.

Here are some popular ones:

1. **Prometheus**: Prometheus is an open-source monitoring and alerting toolkit originally built at SoundCloud. It is designed for reliability, scalability, and flexibility, making it suitable for monitoring cloud environments. Prometheus follows a pull-based model for collecting metrics and supports multi-dimensional data collection and querying.

2. **Grafana**: Grafana is an open-source visualization and analytics platform that can be used in conjunction with Prometheus or other data sources to create dashboards and visualizations for monitoring cloud usage. Grafana supports a wide range of data sources and offers customizable dashboards, alerts, and reporting capabilities.

3. **InfluxDB**: InfluxDB is an open-source time-series database that can be used for storing and analyzing metrics data collected from cloud environments. InfluxDB is optimized for high write throughput and query performance, making it suitable for storing large volumes of time-series data generated by cloud monitoring tools.

4. **Telegraf**: Telegraf is an open-source agent for collecting and reporting metrics data. It supports a wide range of input plugins for collecting data from various sources, including cloud providers, operating systems, and applications. Telegraf can be used to collect metrics data and send it to monitoring and analytics platforms such as Prometheus or InfluxDB.

5. **OpenTelemetry**: OpenTelemetry is an open-source observability framework that provides a set of APIs, libraries, and instrumentation tools for collecting telemetry data from cloud applications and infrastructure. OpenTelemetry supports distributed tracing, metrics collection, and logging, making it suitable for monitoring and troubleshooting cloud environments.

6. **Collectd**: Collectd is an open-source daemon for collecting system performance metrics. It supports a wide range of plugins for collecting data from various sources, including CPU usage, memory usage, disk I/O, and network traffic. Collectd can be used to collect metrics data from cloud instances and send it to monitoring systems for analysis.

5.2 Usage Rating

Usage rating refers to the process of determining the usage charges or fees associated with the consumption of cloud and AI products or services. It involves assigning a monetary value to the quantity of resources or features utilized by customers based on predefined pricing plans or billing models. Usage rating is a crucial component of the billing and invoicing process for cloud and AI products, as it directly impacts the cost incurred by customers.

For cloud products, usage rating typically involves measuring various usage metrics such as compute resources utilization (e.g., CPU usage, memory usage), storage consumption, network bandwidth usage, data transfer volumes, and service-level commitments (e.g., uptime, response time). These usage metrics are then converted into billable units according to the pricing structure defined by the cloud provider, which may include pay-as-you-go pricing, subscription-based models, tiered pricing plans, or usage-based billing.

The usage rating process may vary depending on the specific cloud or AI platform, as well as the pricing policies and billing methods adopted by the service provider. Automated billing systems and usage tracking tools are often employed to accurately capture usage data, calculate charges, generate invoices, and provide customers with transparent billing statements reflecting their usage of cloud and AI resources. Usage rating mechanisms help ensure fair and transparent pricing, enable cost optimization, facilitate billing accuracy, and support customer billing inquiries and auditing processes.

Usage rating for cloud services involves the process of calculating the cost of consumed resources based on predefined pricing models and usage metrics.

A usage rating engine applies the pricing model to the usage data to calculate the cost of consumed resources. This involves mapping the usage metrics to the corresponding pricing rates and performing calculations to determine the total cost.

5.2.1 Rating Factors

The determination of factors for cloud product rating involves multiple considerations due to the complexity and variability of cloud services and usage patterns.

Cloud billing involves multiple dimensions, such as usage-based billing, subscription plans, reserved instances, spot instances, discounts, promotions, and add-on services. Each dimension adds complexity to the billing process and requires consideration in the rating determination.

The determine factors for cloud rating includes:

1. **Usage Metrics**: The amount of compute resources (e.g., CPU, memory), storage space, and network bandwidth utilized by the customer's applications or services on the cloud platform.

   Various usage metrics, such as the duration of resource usage (e.g., hours of compute instances), data transfer volumes (both inbound and outbound), and the number of API requests or transactions processed.

2. **Pricing Plan**: The specific pricing plan or billing model selected by the customer, which may include pay-as-you-go pricing, subscription-based plans, reserved instances, spot instances, or usage-based billing.

3. **Tiered Pricing**: For tiered pricing plans, the level or tier of service utilized by the customer, which determines the applicable rates or discounts based on usage thresholds or volume tiers.

4. **Discounts and Promotions**: Any applicable discounts, promotions, or credits applied to the customer's account, which can influence the final rated amount for cloud usage.

5. **Usage Patterns**: The pattern and frequency of resource usage over time, including peak usage periods, seasonal fluctuations, and usage spikes, which may affect billing calculations and cost projections.

6. **Region and Availability Zone**: Pricing may vary depending on the geographic region and availability zone where resources are deployed. Customers may incur additional charges for data transfer between regions or availability zones.

7. **Service Level Agreements (SLAs)**: Adherence to agreed-upon SLAs regarding uptime, availability, performance, and response times. SLA violations or deviations may impact the final rating result and associated penalties or credits.

5.2.2 Rating Engine

The cloud industry is constantly evolving, with new services, features, and pricing options being introduced regularly. A flexible rating engine provides CSPs with the agility to adapt to changing market trends, customer preferences, and regulatory requirements. It enables rapid experimentation, innovation, and iteration in billing strategies to stay ahead of the competition.

CSPs often adjust their pricing strategies to remain competitive and attract customers. A flexible rating engine enables dynamic pricing adjustments, promotional offers, volume discounts, and custom billing arrangements. It allows for the implementation of complex pricing rules and policies without requiring significant system modifications.

As CSPs scale their operations and expand their customer base, the billing system must be able to handle increasing volumes of usage data and transactions. A flexible rating engine is designed to scale horizontally and accommodate growing demand, ensuring that the billing system remains responsive, reliable, and performant even under high loads.

Designing a flexible rating engine for cloud products involves creating a system that can dynamically calculate usage charges based on various factors and pricing models. Here are some key steps to design such an engine:

1. **Support Multiple Pricing Models**: Accommodate different pricing models such as pay-as-you-go, subscription-based, reserved instances, spot instances, tiered pricing, and custom pricing plans. The rating engine should be able to apply the appropriate pricing model based on customer preferences and contractual agreements.

2. **Dynamic Pricing Rules**: Implement flexible pricing rules that can be easily configured and modified. These rules should allow for adjustments based on factors such as demand fluctuations, promotional offers, volume discounts, and contract terms.

3. **Customizable Billing Policies**: Provide the ability to define customizable billing policies that govern how usage is rated and charged. This may include policies for rounding, minimum charges, overage fees, currency conversion, taxation, and compliance with regulatory requirements.

4. **Integration with Cloud APIs**: Integrate with cloud provider APIs to retrieve usage data, monitor resource consumption, and manage billing-related operations. This

ensures seamless communication between the rating engine and cloud infrastructure.

5. **Scalability and Performance**: Design the rating engine to handle large volumes of usage data and scale horizontally to accommodate growing demand. Optimize performance to ensure timely processing of usage calculations and billing transactions.

6. **Testing and Validation**: Thoroughly test the rating engine under various scenarios to ensure accuracy, reliability, and compliance with business requirements. Validate calculations against expected results and conduct regression testing when making changes or updates.

By following these steps, you can design a flexible rating engine that meets the diverse needs of cloud customers, supports dynamic pricing models, ensures accuracy in usage calculations, and facilitates transparent billing processes.

5.2.3 Estimated Rating

Estimated rating for cloud products refers to the process of predicting or forecasting the expected usage charges that a customer will incur based on their anticipated usage patterns, configuration settings, and historical data. It involves calculating an estimate of the total cost associated with using specific cloud services over a given period, typically before the actual usage occurs.

The purpose of estimated rating is to provide customers with an approximation of their potential expenses, allowing them to plan and budget accordingly. It helps customers make informed decisions about resource allocation, service selection, and cost optimization strategies. Additionally, estimated rating can assist cloud service providers (CSPs) in managing capacity, forecasting revenue, and improving resource allocation based on projected demand.

Realizing estimated rating for cloud products involves implementing a system that can accurately predict the usage charges a customer is likely to incur based on various factors. Here's how you can achieve this:

1. **Data Analysis**: Gather and analyze historical usage data to identify patterns and trends in resource consumption. This data can include metrics such as CPU usage, memory usage, storage usage, network traffic, and other relevant parameters.

2. **Predictive Modeling**: Use statistical techniques and machine learning algorithms to build predictive models that can forecast future usage based on historical patterns. These models can take into account factors such as seasonality, growth trends, and periodic fluctuations in demand.

3. **Service Configuration Analysis**: Understand the specific configurations chosen by the customer for each cloud service, such as instance types, storage options, network settings, and additional features. Associate each configuration with its corresponding cost structure.

4. **Pricing Model Mapping**: Map the customer's chosen pricing model (e.g., pay-as-you-go, reserved instances, spot instances) to the estimated resource consumption. Calculate the cost based on the applicable rates or pricing tiers for each resource type.

5. **Discounts and Promotions**: Incorporate any applicable discounts, promotions, or special offers into the estimation process. Take into account negotiated pricing terms or volume discounts that may apply to the customer's account.

6. **Billing Period Definition**: Determine the billing period or duration for which the estimate is calculated (e.g., hourly, daily, monthly). Ensure consistency in how usage is aggregated and billed across different time intervals.

7. **User Interface**: Provide a user-friendly interface or dashboard where customers can view their estimated usage and associated costs in real-time. Present the information in a clear and understandable format, with the option to drill down into specific details or scenarios.

5.3 Bill & Invoice

The terms "bill" and "invoice" are often used interchangeably, but there are subtle differences between them, especially in the context of billing and accounting:

1. **Bill**:

   - A bill is a formal request for payment issued by a seller or service provider to a customer.

   - It typically outlines the amount owed by the customer for goods or services received.

   - Bills can be issued before, during, or after the provision of goods or services.

   - In some cases, a bill may serve as a statement of account, summarizing charges incurred over a specific period.

2. **Invoice**:

   - An invoice is a specific type of bill that serves as a detailed record of a transaction between a seller and a buyer.

- It itemizes the goods sold or services rendered, including descriptions, quantities, prices, and any applicable taxes or fees.

- Invoices are typically issued after the completion of a sale or the delivery of goods or services.

- They often include payment terms, such as due date, payment methods accepted, and any discounts or late fees.

In summary, while both terms refer to requests for payment, a bill is a broader term that can encompass various types of payment requests, including invoices. An invoice, on the other hand, is a specific type of bill that provides detailed information about a particular transaction between a seller and a buyer.

Once the usage has been rated and the cost calculated, the cloud provider generates a billing statement or invoice for the customer. This statement typically includes detailed information about the consumed resources, usage metrics, pricing rates, and total cost.

In this book, the author treats "bill" and "invoice" as the same concept, referring to the payment request or statement issued to the customer.

5.3.1 Billing Cycle

The billing cycle for cloud services refers to the recurring period during which a customer's usage of cloud resources is measured, billed, and invoiced by the cloud service provider.

The billing cycle repeats on a recurring basis, with new billing cycles beginning immediately following the end of the previous cycle. This allows the cloud service provider to continue measuring and billing the customer's usage of cloud resources on an ongoing basis.

The time zone for the billing cycle in cloud services is typically determined by the cloud service provider. It's commonly based on the location of the provider's headquarters or primary data centers. However, this can vary depending on the provider's policies and the geographical distribution of their customers.

Customers should pay attention to the time zone specified by their cloud service provider for billing purposes to ensure accurate tracking of usage and timely payment of invoices. This information is usually outlined in the provider's billing documentation or customer agreements.

The typical billing cycle for a cloud product often depends on various factors, including the service provider's pricing strategy, customer preferences, and industry standards. However, a common billing cycle for cloud services is monthly billing.

While monthly billing is common, some cloud providers may offer alternative billing cycles, such as quarterly or annually, depending on customer preferences and the nature of the services offered. Additionally, certain types of cloud products, such as on-demand services or pay-as-you-go models, may utilize more frequent billing cycles, such as hourly or daily billing, to reflect usage in real-time. Ultimately, the choice of billing cycle should be based on factors such as customer needs, market expectations, and business objectives.

5.3.2 Bill Generation

The procedure to generate a bill based on rated usage involves several steps:

1. **Aggregation**: Aggregate the rated usage data to generate a summary of charges for each customer or account. This involves consolidating usage records, applying any relevant aggregation rules (such as grouping usage by billing period

or service category), and calculating the total cost for each customer.

2. **Adjustments**: Apply any adjustments or corrections to the rated usage data, such as prorating charges for partial billing periods, applying credits or refunds for service interruptions or downtime, or resolving billing disputes.

3. **Invoice Generation**: Generate the bill or invoice based on the aggregated and rated usage data. The invoice typically includes detailed information about the services consumed, the corresponding charges, any applicable taxes or fees, and payment instructions.

4. **Delivery**: Deliver the bill or invoice to the customer through the preferred communication channel, such as email, online portal, or postal mail. Provide customers with access to their billing information and payment history for transparency and record-keeping purposes.

5.3.3 Bill Splitting

Bill splitting for cloud products refers to the process of dividing the total cost of cloud services or resources among multiple users or departments based on their respective usage or consumption. This approach is often used in shared environments where different entities or users share access to the same cloud infrastructure or services but require separate billing for their usage.

Cloud users often operate in multi-tenant environments where multiple users or departments share the same cloud resources. Bill splitting provides transparency by clearly delineating each user's or department's share of the total costs, allowing them to understand their individual usage expenses.

For organizations with multiple departments or cost centers, bill splitting helps in budget allocation and management. It allows departments to track their own cloud usage costs separately, facilitating better financial planning and resource allocation.

Realizing bill splitting for cloud products involves implementing a mechanism that accurately attributes costs to different users, departments, or projects based on their usage of cloud resources. Here's how to achieve it:

5. **User Identification**: Ensure that the cloud platform can accurately identify individual users, departments, or projects accessing the resources. This may involve integrating with user authentication systems or assigning unique identifiers/ tag to each entity.

6. **Usage Tracking**: Implement robust usage tracking mechanisms to monitor resource consumption at the granular level. Track metrics such as compute hours, storage usage, data transfer, and any other relevant usage metrics for each user or entity.

7. **Cost Allocation Rules**: Define clear and transparent rules for allocating costs based on resource usage. This may include allocating costs proportionally based on usage volume, assigning fixed costs to specific users or departments, or using custom allocation logic tailored to the organization's needs.

8. **Integration with Billing System**: Integrate the usage tracking data with the billing system to generate accurate bills. Ensure that the billing system can apply the defined cost allocation rules and generate separate bills or cost reports for each user or entity.

9. **Customizable Reporting**: Provide users with access to customizable billing reports that clearly show their individual usage and costs. Allow users to filter and view bills based on different criteria, such as time period, resource type, or cost center.

10. **Transparency and Communication**: Maintain transparency by clearly communicating the bill splitting methodology to users and stakeholders. Provide documentation or training on how costs are allocated and how users can interpret their bills.

By implementing these steps, organizations can effectively realize bill splitting for cloud products, enabling accurate cost attribution, budget management, and accountability across different users, departments, or projects.

5.4 Billing Experience

Billing experience refers to the overall customer journey and interaction with the billing process of a product or service. It encompasses all touchpoints, interactions, and perceptions that customers have related to billing, including invoice generation, payment methods, billing inquiries, support interactions, and overall satisfaction with the billing process.

A positive billing experience is essential for customer satisfaction and retention, as it directly impacts how customers perceive the value of the product or service they are paying for. Here are some key elements that contribute to a positive billing experience:

1. **Clarity and Transparency:** Customers appreciate clear and transparent billing practices that provide them with a comprehensive understanding of what they are being charged for, how charges are calculated, and any applicable fees or

taxes. Transparent billing statements and invoices help build trust and credibility with customers.

2. **Ease of Understanding:** Billing documents, such as invoices or statements, should be easy to understand and interpret, even for customers who may not be familiar with financial terminology. Providing clear explanations, itemized details, and visual aids can help customers quickly grasp their billing information.

3. **Convenience and Accessibility:** Customers value convenience and accessibility when it comes to managing their billing accounts. Offering multiple payment methods, online payment portals, automated billing options, and self-service capabilities enable customers to pay bills and manage their accounts conveniently, anytime and anywhere.

4. **Responsive Customer Support:** Prompt and responsive customer support is crucial for addressing billing inquiries, resolving billing disputes, and assisting customers with billing-related issues. Accessible customer support channels, such as phone, email, live chat, or self-service portals, help ensure timely assistance and resolution of customer concerns.

5. **Flexibility and Options:** Providing flexibility and options in billing arrangements, such as different payment plans, billing cycles, or billing preferences, allows customers to tailor their billing experience to their needs and preferences. Offering customizable billing options demonstrates a customer-centric approach and fosters loyalty.

6. **Security and Privacy:** Customers expect their billing information to be handled securely and confidentially. Implementing robust security measures, encryption protocols, and compliance with data privacy regulations help protect

sensitive billing data and instill confidence in customers regarding the security of their financial information.

7. **Proactive Communication:** Proactively communicating with customers about billing-related updates, changes, or upcoming charges helps keep them informed and reduces surprises. Sending reminders for upcoming payments, notifications of billing changes, or alerts for unusual billing activity can improve the overall billing experience.

By focusing on these elements, businesses can create a positive billing experience that enhances customer satisfaction, fosters trust and loyalty, and contributes to long-term customer relationships.

5.4.1 Bill Statement

Bill statements serve as a crucial communication tool between CSPs and their customers. They provide transparency regarding the services used, associated charges, and payment due dates, helping to ensure clarity and trust in the billing process.

Accurate billing is essential for maintaining customer satisfaction and trust. Bill statements enable CSPs to accurately calculate charges based on usage metrics, service plans, and any applicable discounts or promotions, ensuring customers are billed correctly for the services they receive.

Designing a good bill statement for cloud products involves several key considerations to ensure clarity, accuracy, and usability for customers. Here are some steps to design an effective bill statement:

1. **Clear and Concise Format**: Use a clean and organized layout that presents information in a clear and easy-to-understand format. Arrange sections logically and use

headings, subheadings, and bullet points to improve readability.

2. **Detailed Usage Breakdown**: Provide a detailed breakdown of the services used during the billing period, including resource usage metrics such as compute hours, storage capacity, network bandwidth, etc. Clearly itemize each service or resource and specify the quantity consumed.

3. **Cost Breakdown**: Clearly outline the costs associated with each service or resource, including base fees, usage-based charges, taxes, and any applicable discounts or promotions. Break down costs by service type and provide a subtotal for each category.

4. **Usage Metrics and Measurements**: Include relevant usage metrics and measurements for each service or resource, such as the quantity consumed, unit of measurement (e.g., hours, gigabytes), and rate or price per unit.

5. **Billing Period Information**: Clearly state the billing period covered by the statement, including the start and end dates. This helps customers understand the timeframe for which they are being billed and facilitates comparison with previous statements.

6. **Payment Due Date and Instructions**: Clearly indicate the payment due date and provide instructions on how customers can make payment. Include information on accepted payment methods, payment channels, and any additional fees or penalties for late payment.

7. **Customer Account Information**: Display the customer's account information, including account number, billing

address, and contact details. This helps customers identify their account and ensures accurate billing and correspondence.

8. **Usage Trends and Insights**: Optionally, provide usage trends and insights to help customers understand their usage patterns over time. Graphical representations or charts can be used to visualize usage trends and highlight areas of high or unusual consumption.

9. **Support and Contact Information**: Include contact information for customer support, billing inquiries, and technical assistance. This ensures customers know where to turn for help or clarification if they have questions about their bill.

10. **Branding and Brand Identity**: Incorporate branding elements such as the company logo, color scheme, and typography to reinforce brand identity and enhance brand recognition.

By following these guidelines and incorporating customer feedback, CSPs can design bill statements that are informative, transparent, and user-friendly, ultimately improving the customer experience and satisfaction with billing processes.

To meet the needs of customers to understand and manage cloud bills from different perspectives, a flexible billing system can be designed to support querying and aggregating bills based on multiple dimensions.

- **Multi-dimensional querying**: Implement a query function in the billing system that allows customers to filter and query bills based on different dimensions. These dimensions can include region, host instances, network domains, etc., allowing customers to choose the appropriate dimension for their queries.

- **Customizable reports**: Provide customizable report functionality that allows customers to tailor billing reports to their needs. Customers can select the dimensions and metrics they want to display, set filtering conditions, and sorting rules to generate custom reports that meet their requirements.

- **Flexible aggregation**: Implement flexible aggregation functionality that allows customers to aggregate and summarize billing data based on different dimensions. Customers can group, sum, average, etc., billing data as needed to better understand and analyze billing information.

- **Visual presentation**: Provide visualization features to present billing data in charts, tables, etc. Customers can use charts and graphics to analyze trends and correlations in billing data more intuitively.

Through these features and characteristics, customers can understand and manage cloud bills from multiple dimensions, better grasp their consumption, optimize resource usage, and improve cost-effectiveness.

5.4.2 Billing Communication

Billing systems play a critical role in customer communication by sending out invoices, payment reminders, and other billing-related notifications. They provide customers with clear and timely information regarding their financial obligations and payment deadlines.

Billing communication consists of the process of conveying billing-related information between a cloud service provider and its customers.

It encompasses various forms of communication, including invoices, billing statements, notifications, reminders, and customer support interactions.

The primary objectives of billing communication are to:

1. **Inform Customers**: Billing communication informs customers about their usage of services, associated charges, and payment due dates. It provides clarity and transparency regarding the services rendered and the costs incurred.

2. **Facilitate Payments**: Billing communication includes instructions for making payments, such as accepted payment methods, payment deadlines, and billing addresses. It aims to facilitate the payment process and ensure timely payments from customers.

3. **Address Inquiries**: Billing communication addresses customer inquiries, concerns, or disputes related to billing issues. It provides channels for customers to seek clarification, resolve discrepancies, or request assistance with billing-related matters.

4. **Promote Engagement**: Billing communication can serve as an opportunity to engage with customers and promote additional services, upgrades, or special offers. It may include promotional messages, cross-selling suggestions, or loyalty program incentives to encourage customer retention and upselling.

5. **Comply with Regulations**: Billing communication adheres to regulatory requirements and industry standards governing billing practices, data privacy, and consumer protection. It ensures compliance with applicable laws and regulations to protect customer rights and interests.

5.4.2 Bill Dispute

Billing disputes can arise due to discrepancies in usage data, incorrect charges, or misunderstandings about pricing terms. Resolving these disputes in a timely and satisfactory manner requires efficient communication channels, accurate record-keeping, and responsive customer support.

Bill disputes are frequent for cloud products due to several reasons:

- **Complex Pricing Models**: Cloud services often employ complex pricing models with various usage-based charges, tiered pricing, and discounts. Customers may find it challenging to understand their bills, leading to disputes over unexpected charges or discrepancies.

- **Misconfiguration   or   Overprovisioning**: Misconfigurations or overprovisioning of cloud resources can lead to higher-than-expected bills. Customers may dispute charges resulting from unintentional resource usage or inefficiencies in their infrastructure setup.

- **Lack of Transparency**: Some cloud providers may lack transparency in their billing practices, making it challenging for customers to understand how charges are calculated or identify errors in their bills. Without clear and detailed billing information, customers are more likely to dispute charges.

- **Billing Errors**: Billing errors, such as inaccurate metering or calculation mistakes, can occur in the cloud billing process. These errors can result in overbilling or underbilling, leading to disputes between customers and cloud providers.

- **Contractual Discrepancies**: Disputes may arise from discrepancies between the terms outlined in customer contracts and the billing practices implemented by the cloud provider. Customers may challenge charges that they believe are not aligned with the agreed-upon terms.

Resolving bill disputes for cloud products requires a systematic approach to address customer concerns and rectify any billing discrepancies. Here are steps that cloud providers can take to resolve bill disputes effectively:

1. **Customer Communication**: Initiate open and transparent communication with the customer as soon as a billing dispute arises. Listen to their concerns, understand the nature of the dispute, and assure them that their issue will be addressed promptly.

2. **Investigation**: Conduct a thorough investigation into the billing discrepancy to identify the root cause. Review billing records, usage data, and any relevant contractual agreements to determine whether the charges are accurate or if there has been an error.

3. **Clarification and Documentation**: Provide clear explanations and documentation to the customer regarding the disputed charges. Share detailed billing statements, usage reports, and any other relevant information to support your findings and demonstrate transparency.

4. **Resolution Options**: Offer various options for resolving the dispute based on the investigation findings. This may include issuing credits or refunds for overcharged amounts, adjusting billing errors, or providing discounts for future services to compensate for any inconvenience caused.

5. **Negotiation and Compromise**: Engage in constructive negotiation with the customer to reach a mutually acceptable

resolution. Be willing to compromise and find a solution that satisfies both parties while preserving the customer-provider relationship.

6. **Escalation Procedures**: Establish clear escalation procedures for unresolved disputes that cannot be resolved through initial communication and investigation. Designate appropriate escalation points within the organization to handle complex or escalated cases promptly.

7. **Customer Support and Follow-Up**: Provide dedicated customer support throughout the dispute resolution process. Keep the customer informed of progress updates, respond promptly to inquiries, and follow up to ensure that the resolution is satisfactory and the issue is fully resolved.

8. **Continuous Improvement**: Use insights gained from resolving billing disputes to identify areas for improvement in billing processes, systems, and customer communication. Implement measures to prevent similar disputes in the future and enhance overall customer satisfaction.

By following these steps and prioritizing proactive communication and resolution efforts, cloud providers can effectively address billing disputes, uphold customer trust, and maintain positive customer relationships.

5.5 Cost Optimization

Cost optimization for cloud users refers to the process of minimizing expenses associated with using cloud services while maximizing the value derived from those services. This involves various strategies and techniques aimed at achieving the most cost-effective utilization of cloud resources.

In today's competitive landscape, customers have numerous options when it comes to selecting a cloud provider. CSPs that offer comprehensive cost optimization tools are more likely to attract and retain customers by addressing their needs for cost control and transparency.

Offering robust cost optimization tools can differentiate a CSP from its competitors in a crowded market. Customers are increasingly looking for CSPs that not only offer reliable and scalable infrastructure but also provide tools and resources to help them optimize costs and achieve their business objectives more effectively.

Within the realm of cloud cost management, there are two related concepts "FinOps" and "Cost Optimization", usually, FinOps encompasses a broader set of activities beyond just cost optimization, including budgeting, forecasting, chargeback, cost allocation, financial governance, and financial reporting.

Cost optimization specifically focuses on reducing unnecessary cloud spending and maximizing the value obtained from cloud investments. While cost optimization is a key component of FinOps, FinOps encompasses broader financial management practices beyond just optimizing costs.

This chapter primarily focuses on methods and practices related to Cost Optimization.

5.5.1 Unnecessity Identification

"Unnecessity identification" refers to the process of identifying elements, features, or expenses within a system, process, or organization that are unnecessary or redundant. This process is essential for cost optimization and efficiency improvement initiatives, particularly in cloud computing environments where resources are often provisioned dynamically, and costs can quickly accumulate.

Cloud service providers (CSPs) can leverage their expertise and knowledge of cloud infrastructure to help identify unnecessary resources for their customers in several ways:

CSP provide cloud monitoring tools to track resource usage, performance metrics, and activity levels. These tools can help identify resources with low or no utilization over time.

CSPs can continuously monitor the performance of customers' cloud resources, analyzing metrics such as CPU utilization, memory usage, and network traffic. Through performance monitoring, CSPs can identify resources that are consistently underutilized or experiencing low performance, indicating potential candidates for optimization or decommissioning.

Configure alerts and notifications to notify cloud users when resources remain idle or underutilized for an extended period. This can prompt action to either optimize or decommission these resources.

5.5.2 Right-Size the Service

Rightsizing cloud services involves matching the resources allocated to an application or workload with its actual requirements, ensuring optimal performance and cost-efficiency.

Analyze historical usage data to understand the typical workload patterns and resource demands of the customer's applications. Look for trends and patterns that can inform customer for rightsizing decisions.

Implement auto-scaling policies for cloud resources to dynamically adjust capacity based on workload demands. This ensures that customers have the right amount of resources available at any given time, avoiding both underprovisioning and overprovisioning scenarios.

Right-sizing cloud resources presents several challenges that organizations may encounter:

1. **Complexity of Cloud Environments**: Cloud environments can be complex, with a wide range of services, instance types, and configurations available. Understanding how different components interact and determining the optimal resource allocations can be challenging.

2. **Dynamic Workloads**: Workloads in the cloud can be highly dynamic, with fluctuating resource demands over time. Predicting future requirements accurately and ensuring that resources are rightsized to accommodate these fluctuations can be challenging.

3. **Lack of Visibility**: Limited visibility into resource usage and performance metrics can hinder rightsizing efforts. Without comprehensive monitoring and analytics tools, organizations may struggle to identify underutilized or overprovisioned resources.

4. **Data Overload**: Cloud environments generate vast amounts of data related to resource usage, performance metrics, and cost. Analyzing this data to make informed rightsizing decisions can be overwhelming, particularly for organizations without robust analytics capabilities.

5. **Cost Considerations**: Balancing performance requirements with cost considerations is crucial when rightsizing cloud resources. Organizations must carefully assess the trade-offs between performance and cost to ensure that resources are optimized effectively.

6. **Resource Interdependencies**: Resources in a cloud environment are often interconnected, and rightsizing one

component may have implications for others. Understanding these interdependencies and mitigating any potential impacts is essential to avoid disruptions to critical services.

7. **Organizational Silos**: In large organizations, different teams may be responsible for managing different aspects of the cloud environment, leading to siloed approaches to resource management. Collaborating across teams and aligning on rightsizing strategies can be challenging but is essential for success.

8. **Skill and Expertise Gap**: Rightsizing cloud resources requires a combination of technical expertise, data analysis skills, and domain knowledge. Organizations may struggle to find personnel with the necessary skills and experience to effectively rightsize their cloud environment.

Addressing these challenges requires a holistic approach that combines technical solutions, organizational alignment, and ongoing optimization efforts.

5.6 Revenue Assurance

Revenue assurance refers to the process of ensuring that a company accurately captures and collects all revenue owed to it, to discover and prevent any possible revenue leakage.

The goal of revenue assurance is to maximize revenue and profitability while maintaining compliance with regulatory requirements and business standards.

Revenue leakage can occur due to various factors, but two main sources of revenue leakage in businesses are:

1. **Billing Errors:** Billing errors are one of the primary sources of revenue leakage. These errors can result from inaccuracies in the billing process, such as incorrect pricing, billing for services not rendered, underbilling, overbilling, or miscalculations in charges. Common causes of billing errors include manual data entry mistakes, system glitches, outdated pricing information, or misinterpretation of customer contracts or agreements. When billing errors occur, revenue may be lost due to underpayment or non-payment of invoices, leading to revenue leakage.

2. **Fraudulent Activities:** Fraudulent activities pose a significant risk of revenue leakage for businesses. This can include various types of fraud, such as subscription fraud, identity theft, account takeover, payment fraud, or collusion with employees or third parties. Fraudulent activities can result in unauthorized access to services, misuse of resources, non-payment of fees, or manipulation of billing records to conceal fraudulent transactions. Detecting and preventing fraud is essential to mitigate revenue leakage and protect the company's financial interests.

This section discusses how to use AI capabilities for anomaly bill detection and bill reconciliation.

5.6.1 Anomaly Detection

Several AI algorithms can be leveraged for billing anomaly detection, each with its own strengths and suitability depending on the specific requirements and characteristics of the billing data. Here are some common AI algorithms used for billing anomaly detection:

1. **Isolation Forest:** Isolation Forest is an unsupervised machine learning algorithm that is well-suited for detecting anomalies in high-dimensional datasets. It works by isolating instances

in the dataset that are significantly different from the majority of the data points. Isolation Forest is particularly effective for detecting outliers and anomalies in billing data where fraudulent or erroneous transactions may deviate significantly from normal patterns.

2. **One-Class SVM (Support Vector Machine):** One-Class SVM is another unsupervised learning algorithm used for anomaly detection. It learns to identify the normal behavior of data points and then flags instances that deviate from this normal behavior as anomalies. One-Class SVM is suitable for detecting outliers in billing data where anomalies may represent fraudulent activities or billing errors.

3. **Autoencoders:** Autoencoders are a type of neural network architecture used for unsupervised learning and dimensionality reduction. They can be trained to reconstruct input data with minimal loss, and anomalies can be identified by comparing the reconstruction error of input data with the original data. Autoencoders are effective for detecting anomalies in billing data where deviations from normal patterns may indicate fraudulent transactions or billing errors.

4. **Random Cut Forest (RCF):** Random Cut Forest is a streaming algorithm for anomaly detection that works by constructing a forest of random decision trees. It identifies anomalies by measuring the average depth of data points in the trees and flagging instances with unusually short paths as anomalies. RCF is suitable for detecting anomalies in streaming billing data where real-time detection is required.

5. **Deep Learning Models:** Deep learning models, such as convolutional neural networks (CNNs) and recurrent neural networks (RNNs), can also be used for anomaly detection in billing data. These models can learn complex patterns

and relationships in the data and flag instances that deviate significantly from expected patterns as anomalies. Deep learning models are suitable for detecting subtle anomalies in billing data where traditional methods may struggle to capture complex patterns.

It's essential to evaluate the performance of these AI algorithms in the context of the specific billing data and business requirements. Often, a combination of multiple algorithms or ensemble techniques may be used to improve detection accuracy and robustness against different types of anomalies. Additionally, ongoing monitoring and refinement of anomaly detection models are necessary to adapt to changing patterns and emerging fraud schemes in billing data.

5.6.2 Billing Reconciliation

In the market, there are several AI-powered billing reconciliation software solutions available. Here are some examples:

1. **HighRadius Cash Reconciliation:** HighRadius offers a software called Cash Reconciliation, which uses AI technology to automate reconciliation, identify anomalies in bills, and verify them. This software helps businesses speed up the reconciliation process, reduce errors and mistakes, and improve billing management efficiency.

2. **BlackLine Account Reconciliations:** BlackLine provides a solution called Account Reconciliations, which uses AI and machine learning technology to automatically match bills and transaction data, identify potential reconciliation issues, and provide real-time reconciliation reports and analysis.

3. **Sage Intacct Reconciliation:** Sage Intacct is a comprehensive ERP system that offers a module called Reconciliation,

which uses AI and smart algorithms to simplify the billing reconciliation process, improve accuracy, and efficiency.

4. **NetSuite Reconciliation:** NetSuite is a cloud-based ERP system that offers a suite of solutions called Reconciliation Suite, which uses AI and automation tools to speed up the billing reconciliation process and provide real-time reconciliation results and reports.

These software solutions all utilize AI technology to improve the accuracy and efficiency of billing reconciliation, helping businesses save time and costs, and reduce the occurrence of errors.

5.6.3 AI for Assurance

AI (Artificial Intelligence) can play a crucial role in addressing revenue leakage by providing advanced analytics, predictive capabilities, and automation to detect, prevent, and mitigate revenue losses. Here's how AI can address revenue leakage:

1. **Anomaly Detection:** AI algorithms can analyze large volumes of transactional data to identify unusual patterns, discrepancies, or anomalies that may indicate potential revenue leakage. By applying machine learning techniques, AI can learn from historical data and detect outliers, suspicious activities, or irregular billing patterns that require further investigation.

2. **Predictive Analytics:** AI-powered predictive analytics models can forecast future revenue trends, customer behavior, and billing anomalies, enabling businesses to anticipate and prevent revenue leakage before it occurs. By analyzing historical data and identifying predictive indicators, AI helps businesses proactively address revenue risks and optimize revenue generation strategies.

3. **Fraud Detection and Prevention:** AI algorithms can detect and prevent fraudulent activities that may lead to revenue leakage, such as subscription fraud, identity theft, or billing fraud. By analyzing transactional data, user behavior, and other relevant factors, AI can identify fraudulent patterns, flag suspicious activities, and trigger alerts for further investigation or intervention.

4. **Automated Billing Reconciliation:** AI-powered systems can automate the verification of billing data, invoices, and payments to ensure accuracy and completeness. By comparing billing records against contract terms, pricing agreements, and service usage data, AI can detect discrepancies or errors in billing processes and reconcile discrepancies in real-time.

6

SALES

Sales is not a new topic, and there are many theories and methods in the market about how to design and manage mature sales processes. However, due to the unique nature of cloud and artificial intelligence (AI) products, the sales process also has many unique characteristics that cloud service providers (CSPs) need to pay special attention to.

1. **Technical Sales**: Cloud and AI products are typically technical products, and salespeople need to have in-depth product knowledge and industry expertise. They need to be able to engage in deep discussions with technical teams and decision-makers to address customers' technical and business challenges.

2. **Solution Selling**: Cloud and AI products are often not simple single-product sales but solution sales. Salespeople need to understand customer needs and provide targeted solutions to meet specific business requirements.

3. **Long Sales Cycles**: Due to the complexity and higher prices of cloud and AI products, sales cycles are typically longer. Salespeople need to patiently build relationships with customers and provide ongoing support and guidance throughout the sales process.

4. **Customized Sales**: Cloud and AI products often require customized sales and implementation solutions to meet specific customer needs. Salespeople need to be able to adjust sales strategies flexibly and work with customers to develop customized solutions.

5. **Continuous Technical Support**: Sales of cloud and AI products involve not only one-time transactions but also continuous technical support and services. Salespeople need to demonstrate the company's technical support capabilities to customers and ensure that customers receive timely support and assistance after purchase.

6. **Education and Training**: Due to the complexity of cloud and AI products, salespeople need to continuously receive education and training to stay up-to-date with the latest product and industry knowledge. They need to be able to explain the complexity of the product to customers and provide training and support to help customers maximize the potential of the product.

In summary, the sales process for cloud and AI products has its unique characteristics, and salespeople need to have in-depth product and industry knowledge as well as good communication and problem-solving skills. Through a professional sales team and effective sales strategies, cloud service providers can successfully promote and sell their products and achieve business goals.

6.1 Sales Pipeline

The sales pipeline, also known as the sales funnel, represents the stages that a prospect goes through from initial contact to closing a sale. Its primary purpose is to track and manage the progress of leads and opportunities through the various stages of the sales process.

The sales pipeline focuses on the movement of leads and opportunities through predefined stages, such as prospecting, qualification, proposal, negotiation, and closing. It provides visibility into the health of the sales process and helps sales teams prioritize activities and allocate resources effectively.

The outcomes of managing the sales pipeline effectively include a predictable sales process, improved sales forecasting accuracy, better resource allocation, and increased revenue generation through optimized conversion rates and deal closures.

In Chapter 3 of this book, we discussed Customer Nurturing, which, despite sharing similarities with the sales pipeline, differs significantly in its fundamental approach, actions, and outcomes.

While the sales pipeline focuses on managing leads and opportunities through predefined stages to drive conversions and revenue, customer nurturing is centered around building and maintaining relationships with prospects and existing customers over time, with the aim of fostering trust, loyalty, and long-term engagement. The actions and strategies employed in customer nurturing are tailored to deliver personalized content, resources, and support to address individual needs and interests, ultimately leading to outcomes such as increased brand awareness, improved customer satisfaction, and higher retention rates. It's essential to recognize and understand these distinctions to effectively leverage both customer nurturing and the sales pipeline in driving business success.

In this section, we will focus on the main aspects that should be included in the sales pipeline of the cloud product industry and how to manage them effectively.

6.1.1 Lead

A lead is a potential customer or prospect who has shown interest in a company's product or service but has not yet progressed far along the sales pipeline. Leads are typically individuals or organizations that have provided their contact information or engaged with the company in some way, such as filling out a form, subscribing to a newsletter, or downloading a whitepaper. Leads require further nurturing and qualification to determine if they are a good fit for the company's offerings and sales efforts.

Capturing leads for cloud products involves various strategies to attract potential customers and encourage them to express interest in your offerings. Here are some effective methods to capture leads for cloud products:

- Content Marketing: Create high-quality content such as blog posts, whitepapers, case studies, and webinars that provide valuable information related to your cloud products. Offer downloadable resources gated behind lead capture forms to collect contact information from interested prospects.

- Website Optimization: Ensure your website is optimized for lead generation by including clear calls-to-action (CTAs), prominently displaying contact forms, and offering relevant content that encourages visitors to provide their information in exchange for valuable resources or offers.

- Paid Advertising: Utilize online advertising channels such as Google Ads, social media advertising, and display ads to target specific audiences interested in cloud products. Create compelling ad copy and landing pages with clear value propositions to encourage lead submissions.

- Webinars and Events: Host webinars, virtual events, or live workshops to educate prospects about your cloud products and showcase their benefits. Collect attendee information during registration and follow up with leads after the event.

- Free Trials and Demos: Offer free trials or product demonstrations to allow prospects to experience your cloud products firsthand. Require users to sign up or provide their contact details to access the trial or demo, enabling you to capture leads for follow-up.

- Referral Programs: Encourage existing customers, partners, and industry influencers to refer potential leads to your cloud products. Implement referral programs with incentives for successful referrals to incentivize word-of-mouth marketing and lead generation.

- Lead Magnets: Create enticing lead magnets such as e-books, templates, toolkits, or checklists related to cloud technology or industry-specific topics. Promote these lead magnets across various channels to attract leads and capture their information.

- Chatbots and Live Chat: Implement chatbots or live chat on your website to engage visitors in real-time conversations and assist them with inquiries about your cloud products. Use chatbots to qualify leads and capture contact details for follow-up communication.

By incorporating these lead capture strategies into your marketing efforts, you can effectively attract, engage, and convert prospects interested in your cloud products. Tailor your approach based on your target audience, industry, and specific product offerings for optimal results.

Converting leads into opportunities for cloud products involves identifying qualified leads and nurturing them through the sales process until they are ready to engage with your sales team and potentially make a purchase. Here are steps to convert leads into opportunities for cloud products:

1. Lead Qualification: Evaluate leads based on criteria such as budget, authority, need, and timeline (BANT) to determine their suitability as potential customers for your cloud products. Qualify leads who meet your ideal customer profile and show genuine interest in your offerings.

2. Sales and Marketing Alignment: Foster strong collaboration between your sales and marketing teams to ensure a seamless transition of leads from marketing to sales. Define clear criteria for lead handoff and establish communication channels for sharing lead information and feedback.

3. Lead Scoring: Implement a lead scoring system to prioritize leads based on their level of engagement, behavior, and fit with your ideal customer profile. Assign scores to leads based on factors such as website visits, email interactions, content downloads, and webinar attendance.

   AI algorithms can analyze vast amounts of data to identify and score leads based on their likelihood to convert. By considering factors such as online behavior, engagement levels, and demographic information, AI helps sales teams prioritize leads that are most likely to close, allowing them to focus their efforts more effectively.

4. Automated Workflows: Set up automated workflows to track and nurture leads through various stages of the buyer's journey. Use marketing automation tools to send targeted emails, personalized content, and relevant offers to leads based on their interests and actions.

5. Follow-Up and Engagement: Reach out to qualified leads promptly and engage them in meaningful conversations about their challenges, goals, and needs related to cloud products.

Provide valuable insights, answer questions, and offer tailored solutions to demonstrate your expertise and build rapport.

6. Product Demos and Trials: Offer leads the opportunity to experience your cloud products firsthand through product demonstrations, free trials, or proof-of-concept projects. Showcase the features, benefits, and value proposition of your solutions to help leads envision how they can address their specific business needs.

7. Solution Proposals: Create customized solution proposals or quotes that outline the recommended cloud products and services tailored to each lead's requirements and objectives. Highlight key features, pricing details, implementation timelines, and expected outcomes to facilitate decision-making.

8. Relationship Building: Focus on building trust and rapport with leads throughout the sales process. Listen actively to their concerns, address any objections or challenges, and provide ongoing support and guidance to nurture the relationship and move the opportunity forward.

9. Pipeline Management: Keep track of leads' progress through the sales pipeline and regularly review and update their status based on their interactions and engagement with your sales team. Monitor key metrics such as conversion rates, win rates, and sales velocity to identify areas for improvement.

By following these steps and leveraging effective sales and marketing strategies, you can successfully convert leads into opportunities for your cloud products and drive revenue growth for your business. Adapt your approach based on the unique needs and preferences of your target audience to maximize your success.

6.1.2 Opportunity

An opportunity, on the other hand, refers to a qualified lead that has progressed further along the sales pipeline and has a higher likelihood of converting into a paying customer. Opportunities typically arise when a lead meets specific criteria or demonstrates buying intent, such as having a budget, a need for the product or service, and the authority to make purchasing decisions. Sales representatives identify opportunities by conducting thorough qualification processes, engaging in conversations with leads, and understanding their needs and pain points. Once a lead has been qualified as an opportunity, sales efforts focus on nurturing the relationship, addressing any objections, and ultimately closing the sale.

Converting an opportunity into a closed deal for a cloud product involves a systematic process that aligns customer needs with your product offerings, ultimately leading to a successful sale. Here's a typical workflow:

Needs Assessment

Conduct a thorough analysis of the prospect's needs. This may involve discussions, questionnaires, or meetings to understand their business challenges, technical requirements, and desired outcomes.

Cloud and AI solutions can be complex, and clients may not fully understand their own needs or how these technologies can address their challenges. Clients might struggle to articulate their requirements or desired outcomes, especially if they are not familiar with the potential of cloud and AI technologies.

Product Demonstration

Schedule a product demonstration to showcase how your cloud product addresses their specific needs. Tailor the demonstration to highlight features and functionalities that solve their pain points.

Clients may have budget constraints or may not understand the cost-benefit analysis of implementing cloud and AI solutions, requiring detailed explanations and justifications.

Demonstrating the tangible value and ROI of cloud and AI projects can be challenging, especially for more abstract or long-term benefits.

Proposal Submission

Based on the insights gathered from previous steps, prepare a customized proposal. The proposal should detail the product features, implementation plan, pricing, and value proposition tailored to the prospect's requirements.

Ensuring the proposed solutions are compatible with the client's existing IT infrastructure and can be integrated seamlessly.

Tailoring the solution to fit specific business needs, which can vary greatly from one client to another, requires deep technical expertise and can be resource-intensive.

The hype around AI can lead to unrealistic expectations regarding the capabilities and immediate benefits of AI solutions.

Balancing what is technically possible with what can be realistically delivered within a client's timeframe and budget.

With increasing data breaches and cyber threats, clients are understandably concerned about data privacy and security. Addressing these concerns while proposing cloud and AI solutions is crucial.

Ensuring that the proposed solution complies with industry regulations and standards, which can be particularly challenging in highly regulated sectors.

AI can automate the creation of customized proposals based on the specific needs and data collected from potential clients. This not only saves time but also ensures that proposals are highly tailored to each prospect, increasing the likelihood of conversion.

Negotiation

Engage in negotiations with the prospect to address any concerns, adjust terms, or finalize pricing. This step may involve multiple rounds of discussions to reach a mutual agreement.

Closing the Deal

Once the negotiation is successful, proceed to close the deal. This involves signing contracts, finalizing the terms of service, and setting up payment arrangements.

6.1.3 Sales Closure Analysis

The analysis of sales opportunities closure, which ultimately result in either "Closed Won" or "Closed Lost," is crucial for business growth and improvement for several reasons:

- **Identifying Factors of Success**

  Understanding What Leads to Success: Analyzing cases of "Closed Won" can determine the key factors leading to sales success, such as product features, pricing strategy, customer service, or sales approach.

  Replicating Successful Patterns: Once the strategies and methods that are most effective are identified, these best practices can be applied across the sales team and to future sales opportunities.

- **Analyzing Reasons for Failure**

Identifying Causes of Failure: Analysis of "Closed Lost" scenarios helps reveal why sales opportunities failed to convert into deals, whether due to pricing, product mismatch with customer needs, competitors' influence, or issues within the sales process.

Improvements and Adjustments: Understanding the reasons for failure allows a company to adjust its sales strategy, product positioning, or customer communication methods to avoid repeating the same mistakes in the future.

- **Customer Behavior and Market Trends**

Insight into Customer Preferences: Analyzing why some sales opportunities succeed while others fail helps better understand customer preferences and needs in the target market.

Adapting to Market Changes: Regular analysis of successes and failures can reveal market trends and shifts, enabling businesses to quickly adapt and adjust their market strategies.

- **Enhancing Resource Allocation Efficiency**

Optimizing Resource Use: Knowing which types of sales opportunities are more likely to succeed helps businesses allocate marketing and sales resources more effectively.

Improving ROI: By reducing expenditure on opportunities with a low success rate, businesses can enhance overall sales efficiency and investment return.

- **Facilitating Growth and Development of the Sales Team**

    Strengthening Sales Skills: Analysis of both successful and unsuccessful cases provides learning opportunities for the sales team, helping them understand how to improve their sales skills and strategies.

Motivation and Feedback: The results of the analysis can also serve as a basis for providing positive feedback and motivation to the sales team, especially when it clearly demonstrates which behaviors and strategies led to success.

In summary, detailed analysis of "Closed Won" and "Closed Lost" outcomes is an indispensable step in enhancing sales efficiency, optimizing products and services, strengthening customer relationships, and guiding future strategic planning. This analysis helps businesses gain a deep understanding of various aspects of their operations, enabling them to make more informed decisions and achieve sustainable growth.

6.1.4 Sales Forecasting

Accurate sales forecasts enable businesses in the cloud and AI sectors to make informed decisions regarding where to allocate resources and how to prioritize investments in product development and market expansion. Forecasting helps in determining the amount of investment required for research and development, which is crucial for innovation and maintaining competitiveness.

Accurate forecasting also helps in optimizing inventory management and workforce planning, reducing waste, and improving operational efficiency.

With a clear forecast, companies can better negotiate with suppliers and partners, ensuring favorable terms and maintaining a reliable supply chain.

In the fast-paced and innovation-driven cloud and AI industries, sales forecasting is not just a tool for predicting business performance; it is a strategic asset that influences nearly every aspect of business operations. It enables companies to navigate uncertainty, capitalize on emerging opportunities, and sustain long-term growth in a highly competitive environment.

Carrying Out Sales Forecasting for Cloud and AI Products

1. Historical Data Analysis
    Start by analyzing historical sales data to identify trends, patterns, and seasonality in sales of similar products or services. This provides a foundation for forecasting future sales but must be adjusted for market growth, competition, and technological advancements.

2. Market Analysis
    Conduct a thorough market analysis to understand the demand for cloud and AI products, market size, growth rate, and competitive landscape. This includes analyzing potential customer segments, their needs, and how well current products meet those needs.

3. Sales Pipeline Analysis
    Examine the sales pipeline to assess the number of leads, conversion rates, and average deal size. This analysis helps forecast sales based on how many leads are likely to convert into customers.

4. Expert Judgment
   Incorporate insights from sales teams, product managers, and industry experts who understand market trends, customer feedback, and the competitive landscape. Their judgment can adjust forecasts to account for factors not easily quantified, such as market sentiment or upcoming technological breakthroughs.

5. Statistical Methods and AI Models
   Use statistical methods and AI models for more sophisticated forecasts. Machine learning algorithms can analyze complex data sets to identify patterns and predict sales with a high degree of accuracy. These models can incorporate various factors, including economic indicators, industry trends, and online search trends.

6. Continuous Revision and Updating
   Regularly review and update forecasts to reflect new information, market changes, and actual sales performance. This iterative process ensures that forecasts remain relevant and accurate over time.

Sales forecasting for cloud and AI products requires a combination of data analysis, market insight, and technological support. By adopting a comprehensive and adaptive approach, businesses can make informed decisions to drive growth and stay competitive in these dynamic industries.

6.2 CPQ

CPQ stands for Configuration, Pricing, Quotation. It refers to the process or system designed to streamline and automate the configuration, pricing, and quoting processes for complex products or services. CPQ enables sales teams to quickly and accurately generate quotes, proposals, and contracts based on customer requirements and product configurations.

The key components of CPQ software include:

1. **Configuration**: CPQ solutions allow users to configure products or services according to specific customer needs, preferences, and requirements. This may involve selecting features, options, and components from predefined menus or catalogs to create a customized solution.

2. **Pricing**: CPQ software enables dynamic pricing calculations based on factors such as product configurations, discounts, promotions, pricing rules, and customer-specific pricing agreements. It ensures accurate and consistent pricing across all quotes and proposals.

3. **Quoting**: CPQ systems generate professional-looking quotes, proposals, and contracts automatically based on the configured product specifications and pricing rules. They provide templates, branding options, and customization capabilities to create personalized documents tailored to each customer.

6.2.1 Configuration

Cloud products typically offer a wide range of customization options, including different service levels, features, modules, and add-ons. Customers may have unique requirements that necessitate specific configurations to meet their needs. Managing these customization options and ensuring they align with customer requirements can be complex.

The complexity of the sales configuration sheet for cloud products is determined by the following factors:

1. **Variety of Product Specifications:** Cloud products come in various specifications, each catering to different business scenarios and capacity requirements. Clients need to select the appropriate specifications based on their specific needs.

2. **Technical Parameters:** Cloud products have numerous technical parameters, and each product may have different ones. It's crucial to choose the right technical parameters based on the client's business scenario and system requirements.

3. **Compatibility and Rationality Check:** In a single project, multiple cloud products are often required. It's essential to perform compatibility and rationality checks on the configurations of different cloud products to ensure the overall configuration scheme is feasible and optimal.

In summary, the complexity of the sales configuration sheet for cloud products arises from the diverse product specifications, technical parameters, and the need to ensure compatibility and rationality across multiple products within a project.

Software tools can help address the complexity of cloud product configuration sheets in several ways:

- **Template-Based Configuration:** Provide different configuration templates based on various business scenarios and capacity requirements, allowing sales representatives to quickly complete configurations.

- **Compatibility Management:** Manage the compatibility and mutual exclusion relationships between different specifications and parameters of cloud products within the software system, allowing automatic compatibility checks.

- **Configuration Version:** In a sales project for a cloud product, multiple rounds of configuration discussions with the customer are common, where various versions of configurations are provided for their selection. A software system can manage different versions of configurations within the same sales project, highlighting their differences to assist sales managers and customers in making quick judgments and decisions.

- **Configuration Archives:** Maintain archives of configuration solutions from previous projects, enabling quick recommendations for configurations in new projects based on past experiences.

Therefore, an excellent cloud product configuration tool not only provides functionality but also incorporates accumulated knowledge of the cloud product industry.

6.2.2 Pricing

Cloud products typically utilize complex pricing models, which may include usage-based billing, tiered pricing structures, discounts, and promotional offers. Configurations must accurately reflect these pricing considerations based on factors such as usage volume, subscription terms, contract terms, and any applicable discounts or incentives.

Cloud providers may offer discounts or promotions based on factors such as volume commitments, contract length, or usage patterns. Managing these discounts and ensuring they are applied correctly adds complexity to the pricing process.

Pricing for cloud services may vary based on factors such as currency exchange rates or tax regulations in different regions. Managing these considerations adds complexity to pricing calculations, especially for global projects.

The pricing tool for cloud products is typically integrated with the configuration tool to provide CSPs and customers with instant, accurate, and clear pricing information for product solution configurations. This integrated nature enables sales teams to automatically calculate the most suitable prices based on customer needs and selections, ensuring the consistency and accuracy of quotations. Through integrated pricing tools, sales teams can quickly respond to customer demands, offer customized pricing solutions, and facilitate deal closures.

When building a cloud product pricing system, it's important to consider the following points:

1. **Calculation Capability Based on Multiple Pricing Factors:** The system should be able to calculate prices based on various pricing determinants. Given a specific product configuration, the system should query catalog prices, applied discount schemes, assessed usage volumes, etc., to compute estimated total costs for months, quarters, and years, enabling customers to perceive the Total Cost of Ownership (TCO).

2. **Price Comparison Based on Different Configuration Versions:** The system should allow for price comparisons between different configuration versions, empowering customers to make informed choices.

3. **Ability to Provide Price Structure Breakdown and Querying Across Different Dimensions:** The system should offer the capability to break down and query pricing structures across various dimensions such as Region, Host, Domain, or other dimensions, enabling customers to understand the composition of prices.

These considerations ensure that the pricing system provides transparency, flexibility, and clarity to customers during the product selection and purchasing process.

6.2.3 Quotation

Quotation, in the context of sales and pricing, refers to the process of providing a formal estimate or proposal to a potential customer that outlines the cost and terms of a product or service. It typically includes details such as itemized pricing, quantities, discounts (if applicable), payment terms, delivery or implementation timelines, and any other relevant terms and conditions. The purpose of quoting is to provide the customer with a clear understanding of what they will receive and at what cost, facilitating their decision-making process.

Cloud products often have complex pricing structures based on factors like usage, features, and additional services. A quoting tool ensures that quotes provided to customers are accurate and reflect their specific requirements, preventing misunderstandings and disputes.

Quoting manually for cloud products can be time-consuming and error-prone, especially considering the various pricing options and configurations available. A quoting tool automates the process, allowing sales teams to generate quotes quickly and efficiently, ultimately speeding up the sales cycle.

Transparent pricing is essential in building trust with customers. A quoting tool provides visibility into the pricing breakdown, including any discounts, additional fees, and usage-based charges, helping customers understand the value proposition and make informed decisions.

Integrating contract templates into the quoting tool streamlines the sales process by enabling sales representatives to generate quotes and contracts from the same platform. This reduces the need to switch between different systems or applications, saving time and improving efficiency. Contract templates can include standard terms, pricing details, service level agreements (SLAs), and other relevant information. By automating the insertion of customer-specific details into these templates, the quoting tool reduces the risk of manual errors and ensures accuracy in the contract documents.

6.2.4 Guided Selling

Guided selling is a sales technique or approach that involves providing sales representatives with a structured framework or set of tools to effectively lead customers through the buying process. It aims to enhance the sales experience by offering tailored guidance and recommendations based on the customer's needs, preferences, and purchasing behavior. Here are some key aspects of guided selling:

1. **Interactive Questioning**: Guided selling often starts with interactive questioning to understand the customer's requirements, challenges, and objectives. Sales representatives use predefined questions or prompts to gather relevant information and uncover the customer's pain points.

2. **Product Recommendations**: Based on the information collected during the questioning phase, guided selling tools provide tailored product or service recommendations that best meet the customer's needs. These recommendations may include specific features, configurations, or solutions aligned with the customer's requirements.

3. **Visual Aids and Presentations**: Guided selling tools may incorporate visual aids, such as interactive presentations, demos, or product videos, to illustrate key benefits and functionalities of the recommended products or services.

Visual content helps engage customers and reinforce the sales message effectively.

4. **Real-Time Guidance**: Throughout the sales conversation, guided selling tools offer real-time guidance and prompts to help sales representatives navigate complex product catalogs, pricing structures, and objection handling scenarios. This ensures consistency and accuracy in the sales process.

5. **Cross-Selling and Up-Selling Opportunities**: Guided selling techniques leverage customer data and buying patterns to identify cross-selling and up-selling opportunities. Sales representatives are guided to suggest complementary products or upgrades that enhance the value proposition for the customer.

6. **Customized Proposals and Quotes**: Guided selling tools assist sales representatives in creating customized proposals, quotes, or presentations tailored to the customer's specific needs and preferences. Templates and pre-built content modules make it easier to generate professional and compelling sales documents.

7. **Decision Support**: Guided selling provides decision support tools, such as ROI calculators, comparison matrices, and case studies, to help customers evaluate options and make informed purchase decisions. These tools facilitate transparency and build trust throughout the buying process.

AI (Artificial Intelligence) can significantly enhance guided selling for cloud products by leveraging advanced algorithms and data analytics to provide personalized recommendations, streamline the sales process, and improve overall effectiveness. Here's how AI can enhance guided selling for cloud products:

- **Customer Insights**: AI can analyze large volumes of customer data, including past interactions, preferences, and behavior patterns, to gain valuable insights into individual customer needs and preferences. By understanding customers better, AI-powered guided selling tools can tailor recommendations and sales pitches to resonate with each customer's unique requirements.

- **Predictive Analytics**: AI algorithms can predict future buying behaviors and trends based on historical data and real-time inputs. By leveraging predictive analytics, guided selling tools can anticipate customer needs, identify potential opportunities, and proactively recommend relevant products or services before customers even express their requirements.

- **Natural Language Processing (NLP)**: AI-powered NLP technology enables guided selling tools to understand and interpret natural language inputs from customers, such as questions, inquiries, or feedback. This capability allows sales representatives to engage in more conversational interactions with customers, providing prompt and relevant responses to their queries.

- **Recommendation Engines**: AI-driven recommendation engines analyze customer data and product attributes to generate personalized product recommendations in real-time. These recommendations are based on factors such as customer preferences, past purchase history, and similar customer profiles. By offering relevant product suggestions, guided selling tools can help customers discover additional offerings that align with their needs.

- **Dynamic Pricing Optimization**: AI algorithms can optimize pricing strategies dynamically based on various factors such as demand, market conditions, and customer behavior. Guided selling tools powered by AI can adjust pricing recommendations in real-time to offer competitive pricing options that maximize value for both customers and the CSP.

- **Sales Performance Analytics**: AI-powered analytics tools can track and analyze sales performance metrics, identify trends, and uncover areas for improvement in the guided selling process. By providing actionable insights, AI helps sales teams refine their strategies, optimize their approaches, and achieve better results over time.

- **Virtual Sales Assistants**: AI-driven virtual sales assistants can automate routine tasks, provide personalized recommendations, and assist sales representatives throughout the sales process. These virtual assistants can handle inquiries, schedule meetings, generate quotes, and offer guidance, freeing up sales reps to focus on high-value interactions with customers.

AI enhances guided selling for cloud products by leveraging data-driven insights, predictive analytics, natural language processing, and automation capabilities to deliver personalized experiences, drive sales effectiveness, and improve customer satisfaction. By harnessing the power of AI, CSPs can elevate their guided selling efforts and stay ahead in today's competitive marketplace.

6.3 Sales Promotion

In the context of marketing, "promotion" refers to the activities and strategies undertaken to communicate the value of a product, service, or brand to target customers with the goal of increasing sales and enhancing brand awareness. Promotion encompasses various marketing tactics aimed at influencing consumer behavior and driving engagement with the product or brand.

Promotion typically includes a mix of promotional channels and methods, such as advertising, sales promotions, public relations, direct marketing, digital marketing, and personal selling. Each promotion method serves a specific purpose and can be tailored to reach different audience segments and achieve specific marketing objectives.

Sales promotion refers to the set of activities aimed at stimulating purchasing behavior or accelerating the sales of a product or service. Unlike other promotional methods that focus on building brand awareness or long-term brand equity, sales promotion strategies are often short-term initiatives designed to achieve immediate results.

This chapter delves into various techniques and tactics employed in sales promotion, such as discounts, coupons, rebates, loyalty programs. The primary focus is on strategies that directly influence buyer behavior at the point of sale or during the decision-making process. Through effective sales promotion, companies seek to attract new customers, retain existing ones, increase sales volume, and gain a competitive edge in the market.

In a crowded market like the cloud industry, where numerous providers offer similar services, sales promotions can help companies differentiate their offerings. Unique promotions, discounts, or special offers can attract potential customers and set a company apart from its competitors.

Sales promotions play different yet significant roles in various stages of the customer lifecycle, serving as vital tools for CSP business development.

- **Customer Acquisition:** Sales promotions can be effective in acquiring new customers by incentivizing them to try out a cloud product or service. For example, offering a limited-time free trial or a discounted introductory offer can entice potential customers to sign up and experience the value of the product firsthand.

- **Customer Retention:** Promotions are not only useful for attracting new customers but also for retaining existing ones. Loyalty rewards programs, special discounts for long-term customers, or exclusive offers for existing users can encourage customer loyalty and reduce churn rates.

- **Boosting Sales:** Sales promotions are designed to stimulate immediate action from customers, leading to an increase in sales volume within a short period. This can be especially beneficial for cloud companies looking to meet sales targets or drive revenue growth.

- **Market Expansion:** By offering promotions that target specific market segments or customer demographics, cloud companies can expand their market reach and penetrate new customer segments. Promotions tailored to different industries, geographical regions, or customer personas can help attract diverse clientele.

- **Product Launches and Upgrades:** When introducing a new cloud product or launching an upgraded version, sales promotions can generate buzz, create excitement, and drive adoption among target customers. Promotional offers during product launches can incentivize early adopters and accelerate the product's market penetration.

Overall, sales promotion strategies are instrumental in achieving various business objectives, including increasing market share, driving revenue growth, improving customer loyalty, and staying ahead of competitors in the dynamic cloud industry.

We will introduce several different methods of promotions, along with their design strategies and application methods.

6.3.1 Discounts

Discounts refer to reductions in the price of a product or service offered by a seller to attract customers, increase sales, or promote certain products. Discounts can take various forms, such as percentage discounts, fixed amount discounts, volume discounts, seasonal discounts. They are commonly used in sales and marketing strategies to incentivize customers to make purchases.

Cloud service providers (CSPs) can typically utilize the following different forms of discounts when promoting cloud products and driving sales:

- **Volume Discounts:** Offering discounts based on the quantity of cloud services or AI products purchased. This encourages customers to buy in bulk, leading to higher sales volumes.

- **Usage-based Discounts:** Providing discounts based on the amount of usage or consumption of cloud resources or AI services. This incentivizes customers to use more of the offered services, leading to increased revenue for the provider.

- **Contractual Discounts:** Offering discounts for customers who sign long-term contracts or commit to using the services for an extended period. This provides stability for the provider and assures a steady stream of revenue.

- **Bundled Discounts:** Offering discounts when customers purchase a bundle of related cloud services or AI products together. This encourages customers to buy more comprehensive solutions and enhances the value proposition.

- **Promotional Discounts:** Providing temporary discounts or special offers during promotional campaigns or events. This creates a sense of urgency and encourages customers to make purchases within a specific timeframe.

- **Upgrade Discounts:** Offering discounts to existing customers who upgrade their current subscription or service plan to a higher-tiered offering. This incentivizes customers to access more advanced features or capabilities.

- **Loyalty Discounts:** Providing discounts or rewards to loyal customers based on their continued patronage or usage of the cloud services or AI products over time. This fosters customer retention and strengthens the relationship between the provider and the customer.

- **Referral Discounts:** Offering discounts to customers who refer new clients or businesses to the cloud service provider or AI product vendor. This incentivizes word-of-mouth marketing and expands the customer base.

The suitability of each type of discount may vary depending on the business model, target market, and specific objectives of the cloud service provider or AI product vendor.

6.3.2 Coupons

A coupon is a promotional document or code that entitles the holder to a discount or special offer when purchasing a product or service. Coupons are often distributed by businesses as part of their marketing strategies to attract customers, stimulate sales, and build brand loyalty.

In the context of cloud and AI products, coupons can be digital or physical vouchers that customers can redeem to receive discounts on subscription plans, usage fees, or additional services offered by cloud service providers (CSPs). These coupons may be distributed through various channels such as email marketing campaigns, social media promotions, or partner collaborations.

Customers typically enter or apply the coupon code during the checkout process when purchasing cloud services online. The discount associated with the coupon is then applied to the total purchase amount, providing customers with cost savings and incentives to engage with the CSP's offerings.

Here are several business scenarios where coupons can be effectively used in the selling of cloud products:

1. **Customer Acquisition:** Offer coupons with discounts or free trials to attract new customers who may be hesitant to try cloud products for the first time. For example, provide a "50% off your first month" coupon to incentivize sign-ups.

2. **Promotion of New Features or Upgrades:** When launching new features or upgrades to existing cloud products, provide coupons to existing customers for a limited-time discount on upgrading to the enhanced version.

3. **Seasonal Promotions:** Run seasonal promotions offering discounts or special offers during holidays or peak business seasons. For instance, offer a "back-to-school" coupon with discounted rates on cloud storage for students and educators.

4. **Partner Collaborations:** Collaborate with partners or affiliates to distribute co-branded coupons, expanding reach and attracting new customers through partner channels. For example, team up with a software provider to offer a bundled package with a coupon for discounted cloud services.

5. **Customer Retention:** Use coupons as a retention strategy by offering discounts or bonus features to existing customers upon contract renewal or as a reward for long-term loyalty.

6. **Referral Programs:** Implement a referral program where existing customers receive coupons or account credits for referring new customers to the cloud product. This incentivizes word-of-mouth marketing and customer advocacy.

7. **Event Sponsorships:** Sponsor industry events or conferences and distribute coupons to attendees, offering exclusive discounts or access to premium features for those who sign up during the event.

8. **Abandoned Cart Recovery:** Send personalized coupons to customers who abandoned their cart during the checkout process, encouraging them to complete their purchase with a limited-time discount.

By strategically using coupons in these various business scenarios, cloud product sellers can drive customer acquisition, retention, and engagement while maximizing sales opportunities and staying competitive in the market.

6.3.3 Rebates

Rebates are a type of promotion method where customers receive a partial refund of the purchase price after completing a specified action, such as making a purchase, subscribing to a service, or meeting certain criteria.

Unlike discounts and coupons, rebates occur after the purchase and usage of a product. Typically, CSPs set certain criteria, such as reaching a certain quantity or amount in product orders or achieving a specific billing amount for a postpaid product in a month, to qualify for rebates. Rebates can take the form of cashback or coupon returns.

Rebates can be applied in various business scenarios for cloud products. One such scenario is when a customer commits to a long-term contract or a large volume purchase of cloud services. For example, if a customer agrees to a three-year subscription for a significant number of virtual machines or storage capacity, they may be eligible for a rebate based on the actual staying period or usage volume or final bill. This incentivizes customers to make larger commitments, leading to increased revenue for the cloud service provider and potentially locking in customers for an extended period.

In traditional approaches, rebates typically require customers to manually submit applications to receive corresponding cashback or coupons. In the cloud industry, to simplify customer operations, once customers meet the specified conditions, rebate issuance is generally triggered automatically by the system.

6.3.4 Points-based system

Points-based systems are a type of loyalty program where customers earn points for their purchases or other interactions with a business. These points accumulate over time and can be redeemed for rewards, discounts, or other incentives offered by the business.

Here's how a typical points-based system works:

1. Accrual of Points: Customers earn points for each qualifying purchase they make. The number of points earned may be based on the dollar amount spent, with customers earning a certain number of points per dollar.
2. Redemption of Points: Once customers have accumulated a sufficient number of points, they can redeem them for rewards. These rewards may include discounts on future

purchases, free products or services, coupons, or other incentives.

3. Tiered Programs: Some points-based systems may have tiered levels of membership, where customers unlock additional benefits or perks as they reach higher point thresholds. This encourages customers to continue engaging with the business to achieve higher status levels.

4. Points Expiry: In some cases, points may have an expiration date, encouraging customers to redeem them within a certain timeframe to avoid losing their value.

5. Promotions and Bonuses: Businesses may offer promotions or bonuses to help customers accumulate points more quickly. For example, they may offer double points for purchases during a specific time period or for buying certain products.

Overall, points-based systems are a popular way for businesses to reward customer loyalty, incentivize repeat purchases, and increase customer engagement.

Points-based systems can be applied to cloud and AI products to incentivize customer loyalty and encourage ongoing engagement. Here's how such a system could be implemented for these types of products:

1. **Usage-Based Points**: Customers can earn points based on their usage of cloud and AI services. Points could be awarded for actions such as deploying new instances, utilizing AI algorithms, processing data volumes, or accessing premium features.

2. **Subscription-Based Points**: Points can also be awarded based on subscription tiers or levels. Higher-tier subscribers could earn more points per unit of usage or receive bonus points as a reward for their loyalty.

3. **Referral Program**: Customers could earn points for referring new clients to the cloud or AI platform. This incentivizes existing users to promote the product to their networks, leading to organic growth.

4. **Training and Education**: Points can be awarded for completing training modules, attending webinars, or participating in educational events related to the cloud or AI services. This encourages users to deepen their understanding of the platform and its capabilities.

5. **Community Engagement**: Points could be earned for participating in user forums, providing feedback, or submitting feature requests. This fosters a sense of community among users and encourages collaboration and knowledge sharing.

6. **Special Promotions**: The platform can offer special promotions where users can earn bonus points for specific actions, such as upgrading their subscription plan, renewing their contract early, or trying out new features.

By implementing a points-based system tailored to the cloud and AI industry, businesses can incentivize desired behaviors, reward customer loyalty, and increase engagement with their products and services.

6.4 Agreement

Agreements are essential for cloud products sales management.

Agreements establish the legal framework for the relationship between the cloud service provider (CSP) and the customer. They outline the rights, obligations, and responsibilities of both parties, helping to mitigate legal risks and disputes.

Agreements define the scope of services provided by the CSP, including the features, functionalities, and limitations of the cloud products. They specify the rights to use the services, any restrictions or usage policies, and the conditions for accessing and managing the resources.

Agreements detail pricing structures, payment terms, and billing arrangements for the cloud services. They clarify the costs associated with the services provided, including any recurring fees, usage charges, or additional expenses, ensuring transparency and preventing misunderstandings.

Agreements specify the service level expectations, including performance standards, uptime guarantees, and support levels. Clear SLAs (Service Level Agreements) ensure that customers understand what to expect from the cloud service and provide assurance of quality and reliability.

Agreements address data protection and security measures, including data privacy, confidentiality, and compliance with relevant regulations (e.g., GDPR, HIPAA). They outline how customer data will be handled, stored, and protected, helping to build trust and confidence in the CSP's security practices.

Agreements outline the terms and conditions for termination, renewal, and extension of the contract. They specify the notice periods, termination procedures, and any penalties or consequences for early termination, providing clarity on the process for ending or renewing the agreement.

In summary, agreements are important for cloud products sales management because they establish the legal, financial, operational, and security parameters of the relationship between the CSP and the customer. By clearly defining rights, obligations, and expectations, agreements provide a framework for delivering and consuming cloud services effectively while protecting the interests of both parties.

6.4.1 Enterprise Agreement

An enterprise agreement, in the context of business and commercial transactions, typically refers to a contractual arrangement between a vendor or service provider (such as a cloud service provider) and a large organization or enterprise customer. This type of agreement outlines the terms and conditions under which the vendor will provide its products or services to the enterprise customer.

Key features of an enterprise agreement may include:

1. **Scope of Services**: Defines the specific products or services being provided by the vendor to the enterprise customer. This could encompass a range of offerings, such as software licenses, cloud computing services, support and maintenance, professional services, etc.

2. **Pricing and Payment Terms**: Outlines the pricing structure, payment terms, and billing arrangements for the products or services. It may include details about pricing tiers, volume discounts, payment schedules, invoicing procedures, and any additional fees or charges.

3. **Duration and Renewal**: Specifies the duration of the agreement (e.g., term length, start date, end date) and provisions for renewal or extension. This ensures clarity regarding the contractual commitment period and any options for continuing the relationship beyond the initial term.

4. **Terms and Conditions**: Sets forth the rights, obligations, and responsibilities of both parties. This includes provisions

related to service levels, performance guarantees, warranties, intellectual property rights, confidentiality, data security, compliance, and legal jurisdiction.

5. **Usage Rights and Entitlements**: Defines the rights of the enterprise customer to access and use the vendor's products or services. It may include details about authorized users, license metrics, permitted usage scenarios, restrictions on use, and any conditions for transferring or sublicensing rights.

6. **Support and Maintenance**: Describes the vendor's obligations to provide support, maintenance, and updates for the products or services covered by the agreement. This could include service level agreements (SLAs), response times, escalation procedures, and access to technical assistance.

7. **Termination and Exit Provisions**: Specifies the circumstances under which either party may terminate the agreement, as well as the procedures and consequences associated with termination. It may address issues such as early termination fees, data extraction and migration, post-termination support, and transition assistance.

Enterprise agreements are often negotiated directly between the CSP and the enterprise customer, taking into account the unique requirements, preferences, and circumstances of both parties. They provide a framework for establishing a long-term relationship and are designed to accommodate the scale, complexity, and specific needs of large organizations.

In the cloud industry, customers can derive several benefits from enterprise agreements:

- **Cost Savings**: Enterprise agreements often provide volume discounts or preferential pricing based on the scale of the customer's commitment. This can lead to significant cost savings compared to standard pricing models, especially for large organizations with substantial cloud usage.

- **Predictable Budgeting**: Enterprise agreements typically offer fixed pricing and terms over an extended period, providing customers with predictability and stability in their IT budgets. This allows organizations to plan more effectively and avoid unexpected cost fluctuations.

- **Streamlined Procurement**: Enterprise agreements streamline the procurement process by standardizing terms and conditions, reducing administrative overhead, and simplifying contract negotiations. This efficiency saves time and resources for both the customer and the cloud service provider.

- **Enhanced Support**: Many enterprise agreements come with elevated support levels or dedicated account management services, providing customers with priority access to technical assistance, troubleshooting, and strategic guidance. This high-touch support enhances the customer experience and accelerates problem resolution.

- **Scalability and Flexibility**: Enterprise agreements often offer flexibility to scale services up or down in response to changing business demands. This scalability allows customers to adjust their cloud usage dynamically without incurring penalties or renegotiating contracts, providing agility and efficiency.

To effectively support enterprise agreements in the cloud industry, a robust system is needed that can handle various aspects of contract management, pricing, billing, provisioning, and customer relationship management. Here are some key components of the system:

1. **Contract Management System**: A centralized platform for managing enterprise agreements, including contract creation, negotiation, approval workflows, version control, and storage. This system should allow easy access to contract terms, conditions, and commitments.

2. **Pricing and Quoting Tools**: Tools that facilitate the pricing and quoting process for enterprise agreements, enabling sales teams to generate accurate quotes based on customer requirements, volume commitments, and pricing tiers. These tools should support complex pricing structures and provide visibility into discounts and incentives.

3. **Billing and Invoicing System**: A billing system capable of handling the billing complexities associated with enterprise agreements, such as tiered pricing, usage tracking, invoicing at scale, and customization of billing cycles. The system should generate detailed invoices that reflect the agreed-upon terms and pricing.

4. **Order Management System**: An order management system to process and fulfill orders related to enterprise agreements, including provisioning of cloud services, activation of subscriptions, and allocation of resources according to customer specifications.

5. **Customer Relationship Management (CRM) System**: A CRM system to manage customer interactions, track sales opportunities, and maintain a comprehensive view of customer accounts. This system should capture customer preferences, history, and engagement data to support ongoing relationship management.

By leveraging a comprehensive system that encompasses these components, cloud service providers can effectively support enterprise agreements, streamline operations, and deliver value-added services to their customers.

6.4.2 Subscription Agreement

A subscription agreement is a contract between a CSP and a customer that outlines the terms and conditions of the subscription service being provided. It establishes the rights, responsibilities, and obligations of both parties regarding the use of the subscribed services.

An enterprise agreement and a subscription agreement are both types of contracts used in the context of providing services, including cloud services, but they serve different purposes and cover different aspects of the service relationship. Here are the key differences between the two:

1. **Scope and Usage**:

    *   **Enterprise Agreement**: An enterprise agreement is a comprehensive contract negotiated between a service provider and a large enterprise customer. It typically covers a wide range of services, products, and terms customized to meet the specific needs of the enterprise. Enterprise agreements are usually long-term contracts and may involve significant commitments from both parties.

    *   **Subscription Agreement**: A subscription agreement is a standard contract used to govern the provision of a specific service to an individual or organization. It outlines the terms and conditions of the subscription service, including pricing, service levels, usage rights, and other relevant details. Subscription agreements are generally more standardized and may apply to multiple customers subscribing to the same service offering.

2. Scale and Complexity:

- **Enterprise Agreement:** Enterprise agreements are typically more complex and involve larger-scale deployments, as they are tailored to the unique requirements of the enterprise customer. These agreements may cover multiple services, locations, user groups, and other variables, requiring extensive negotiation and customization.

- **Subscription Agreement:** Subscription agreements are generally simpler and more straightforward, focusing on the terms specific to the subscribed service. While they may include options for customization or add-on services, subscription agreements are designed to be more standardized and easier to manage for smaller-scale deployments.

3. Duration and Flexibility:

- **Enterprise Agreement:** Enterprise agreements often have longer durations, spanning multiple years, to provide stability and predictability for both parties. They may also include provisions for flexibility and scalability to accommodate changes in the enterprise's needs over time, such as additional services, users, or locations.

- **Subscription Agreement:** Subscription agreements typically have shorter durations, such as monthly or annual terms, with options for renewal. They offer customers greater flexibility to adjust their subscription levels, add or remove services, and scale usage up or down based on their evolving requirements.

4. **Negotiation and Customization**:

- **Enterprise Agreement**: Enterprise agreements involve extensive negotiation and customization to address the specific needs, preferences, and objectives of the enterprise customer. These agreements may include special pricing, volume discounts, service bundles, and other incentives tailored to the enterprise's unique circumstances.

- **Subscription Agreement**: Subscription agreements are generally less negotiable and more standardized, with predefined terms and pricing structures. While customers may have some flexibility to choose among available subscription options, the terms are typically set by the service provider and may be less subject to negotiation.

In summary, enterprise agreements are comprehensive, customized contracts negotiated between service providers and large enterprise customers, covering a wide range of services and terms. Subscription agreements, on the other hand, are standardized contracts used for individual or small-scale subscriptions to specific services, with simpler terms and shorter durations.

6.4.3 Agreement Fulfillment

Agreement fulfillment refers to the process of fulfilling the terms and conditions outlined in a contractual agreement between parties. In the context of cloud services, agreement fulfillment involves delivering the agreed-upon services, features, and support to the customer according to the terms specified in the service agreement or contract.

Agreement fulfillment is crucial for business success of cloud service providers (CSPs).

Fulfilling the terms of the agreement ensures that customers receive the services and support they expect. This leads to higher satisfaction levels, which are essential for retaining customers and fostering positive relationships.

Consistently delivering on promises builds trust and enhances the CSP's reputation in the market. Positive word-of-mouth referrals and testimonials from satisfied customers can attract new clients and contribute to business growth.

Enterprise agreements often involve complex terms and conditions tailored to the specific needs of large organizations. Similarly, subscription agreements may contain intricate pricing structures, usage limits, and renewal terms. Managing and interpreting these complexities accurately can be challenging for CSPs.

In the cloud industry, the fulfillment of agreements often involves paying attention to the following points:

1. **Billing Accuracy**: Ensuring that billing and invoicing are done according to the discounts specified in the agreement. Both enterprise agreements and subscription agreements often entail complex discount schemes, including cross-product discounts based on a customer's total usage or consumption across different products. This requires robust measurement and billing systems from the CSP.

2. **Obligation Monitoring**: Monitoring the obligations that customers should fulfill in real-time and accurately, to initiate penalty measures when necessary. Enterprise agreements may offer customers high and flexible discount schemes but also impose consumption requirements, such as specific product quantities, usage levels, or configurations. CSP systems should be able to retrieve this information in real-time from ordering, metering and billing systems to determine

whether customers have fulfilled their obligations and initiate penalty measures such as supplementary billing or discount downgrade as per the terms.

3. **Notification of Key Events**: Notifying relevant stakeholders, such as the sales representatives responsible for the customer, about key events and milestones in agreement fulfillment. This ensures timely follow-up on agreement performance and necessary actions to maintain a healthy business relationship.

By addressing these points, CSPs can effectively manage agreement fulfillment, uphold agreement commitments, and foster positive relationships with their customers.

7

PARTNER

Partners play an important role in the success of Cloud Service Providers (CSPs) for several reasons, enhancing their capabilities, reach, and overall market position.

Through partnerships, CSPs can offer a broader range of products and services by integrating their cloud solutions with partners' technologies or services. This enables CSPs to meet a wider array of customer needs and preferences, making their offerings more attractive and competitive.

Partners help CSPs expand their market reach to new geographic areas and industry sectors without the need for significant investment in new infrastructure or sales offices. They bring an existing customer base that CSPs can tap into, accelerating market penetration and growth.

Partners often bring specialized knowledge and expertise in specific markets, industries, or technologies. This expertise can be leveraged to develop tailored solutions that address unique customer challenges, enhancing the value proposition of the CSP's offerings.

For CSPs, developing a strong partner ecosystem is not just about outsourcing certain functions or filling gaps in their offerings; it's a strategic approach to growing their business, enhancing their market competitiveness, and creating more value for their customers. Partnerships enable CSPs to leverage external expertise, reach, and resources, which can be pivotal in achieving long-term success in the cloud industry.

This chapter will discuss the selection and management methods of three different types of partners in the cloud computing industry: **product partners, sales partners, and service partners**. It includes content on how to choose partners, how to define the work interfaces with partners, and how to motivate them.

7.1 Product Partner

Cloud Service Providers (CSPs) need product partners for several strategic and operational reasons. Product partners can include software developers, hardware manufacturers, or providers of complementary technologies that enhance the CSP's offerings.

1. **Expanding Product Portfolio**: Partnering with companies that offer complementary products or services allows CSPs to expand their product portfolio. This enables them to provide a more comprehensive solution to their customers, covering a wider range of needs without having to develop these products or services internally.

2. **Enhancing Technical Capabilities**: Product partners often bring specialized technical capabilities that can enhance the CSP's offerings. This can include advanced analytics, security features, or industry-specific solutions. By integrating these capabilities, CSPs can offer more competitive and technically sophisticated services.

3. **Speed to Market**: Developing new technologies and solutions in-house can be time-consuming. Collaborating with product partners can significantly reduce time to market for new offerings, allowing CSPs to respond more quickly to emerging trends and customer demands.

4. **Cost Efficiency**: Leveraging the products and services of partners can be more cost-efficient than developing everything in-house. It allows CSPs to focus their investments on core competencies while still expanding their offerings through partnerships.

5. **Innovation Through Collaboration**: Working with product partners can foster innovation. Partnerships can lead to the development of new and unique solutions that combine the strengths of both parties, offering customers innovative solutions that they cannot find elsewhere.

In essence, product partners are crucial for CSPs to enhance their service capabilities, accelerate growth, and stay competitive in the rapidly evolving cloud computing market. They enable CSPs to meet the diverse and changing needs of their customers more effectively and efficiently.

7.1.1 Partner Model

For Cloud Service Providers (CSPs), choosing the model of collaboration with product partners is a crucial strategic decision that affects their product and service range, market positioning, and customer experience. CSPs can opt to collaborate with different types of partners, including OEM (Original Equipment Manufacturer), ODM (Original Design Manufacturer), and OBM (Original Brand Manufacturer), each with its unique advantages and considerations. Here's an overview of these three models and what they mean for CSPs:

OEM (Original Equipment Manufacturer)

- **Collaboration Model**: OEM stands for Original Equipment Manufacturer. In the context of Cloud Service Providers (CSPs), an OEM refers to a company that manufactures products or components that are used by another company (in this case, the CSP) to be sold under the purchasing company's brand name. OEMs typically focus on the production side of things, creating hardware or software according to the specifications provided by their clients.

- **Advantages**: By partnering with OEMs, CSPs can leverage the manufacturing capabilities and economies of scale of the OEM to obtain cost-effective solutions.

OEMs often have established quality control processes and certifications, ensuring that the products they manufacture meet high standards of quality and reliability.

Partnering with OEMs allows CSPs to focus on their core competencies, such as cloud infrastructure, services, and customer support, rather than on manufacturing hardware or developing software in-house.

ODM (Original Design Manufacturer)

- **Collaboration Model**: ODM stands for Original Design Manufacturer. This term refers to companies that design and manufacture a product as specified and eventually branded by another firm for sale. Such companies allow the brand firm to produce either a component or the entire product while avoiding the expenses and complexities associated with the R&D, design, and manufacturing processes.

- **Advantages**: ODMs provide CSPs with the ability to have products designed according to their specific requirements, allowing for unique features or performance characteristics that can differentiate their offerings in the market.

ODM partnerships can foster innovation by combining the ODM's product design and manufacturing expertise with the CSP's industry knowledge and market insights, leading to the development of innovative and competitive cloud solutions.

OBM (Original Brand Manufacturer)

- **Collaboration Model**: OBM stands for Original Brand Manufacturer. This term refers to companies that design, manufacture, and sell products under their own brand name. Unlike OEMs or ODMs, which manufacture products to be branded and sold by other companies, OBMs take full control of the product lifecycle, including research and development, production, marketing, and sales. In the context of Cloud Service Providers (CSPs), partnering with an OBM means incorporating products or services developed and branded by the OBM into the CSP's offerings.

- **Advantages**: Partnering with well-known OBMs can leverage their brand recognition and customer trust, enhancing the CSP's own offerings with products known for their quality and reliability.

   OBMs are typically invested in the continuous improvement and innovation of their products to maintain their brand reputation, which means CSPs can benefit from high-quality and technologically advanced products.

   OBMs often provide extensive support and warranties for their products, ensuring CSPs can offer reliable services to their customers with minimized risk.

The choice of collaboration model depends on the CSP's strategic goals, market positioning, and the type of relationship they wish to establish with their customers. By partnering with different types of product partners, CSPs can more flexibly meet the diverse needs of the market, drive innovation, and gain a competitive edge in a highly competitive market.

7.1.2 Product Information

To effectively consolidate product information from partners into their own product management systems, Cloud Service Providers (CSPs) need to implement a comprehensive set of technology solutions and process management strategies.

Standardize Product Information

As discussed in section 2.1.1 of the book, due to the vastness of cloud product specifications, it is recommended to use SKUs (Stock Keeping Units) as the standard data structure for management. Similarly, for products from partners, managing them using an SKU-centric data structure is also advisable. This approach facilitates seamless integration and amalgamation with the CSP's own product data structure, enabling unified and automated processing in pricing, quoting, ordering, and accounting stages.

Using SKUs as a core data structure offers several advantages:

1. **Standardization**: SKUs provide a standardized way to refer to each unique product or service, simplifying the management of diverse product offerings from different partners.

2. **Integration**: SKU-based management allows for easier integration of partner products into the CSP's existing product catalog, making it more straightforward to present a cohesive product lineup to customers.

3. **Automation**: By standardizing on SKUs, CSPs can more easily automate various business processes, including product

ordering, inventory management, billing, and more, reducing manual effort and increasing efficiency.

4. **Accuracy**: Using SKUs helps ensure accuracy across different systems and processes by providing a unique identifier for each product variant, minimizing the risk of errors in product selection, pricing, and order fulfillment.

5. **Analytics**: An SKU-centric approach enables detailed analytics and reporting, allowing CSPs to track sales, performance, and trends at a granular level, both for their own products and those of their partners.

Integrate Technology Platforms

Integrating a Product Management Platform with peer systems from product partners involves a series of steps designed to ensure seamless data flow, compatibility, and functionality across different platforms. This integration is crucial for cloud service providers (CSPs) to manage their product offerings effectively, including those from partners, ensuring accurate pricing, quoting, ordering, and billing processes.

Determine which data points need to be shared between the systems, such as product specifications, SKUs (Stock Keeping Units), pricing, and availability.

Utilize Application Programming Interfaces (APIs) for real-time data exchange. APIs allow for direct communication between systems, enabling automated updates and transactions.

In cases where direct API integration is not feasible, consider using middleware solutions that can translate and transfer data between systems with different formats.

Create comprehensive documentation of the integration process, data mappings, and workflows is very important, and ensure relevant staff are trained on the new integrated system operations, focusing on changes to processes or workflows.

Self-Service for Product Management

Providing a self-service tool for product partners to manage their own products is a strategic move that can streamline operations, enhance partner relationships, and improve the accuracy and timeliness of product information.

7.1.3 Offer Integrating

Integrating a partner's product into a Cloud Service Provider's (CSP's) offerings presents several challenges. These challenges span technical, pricing, operational, strategic, and market-related areas. Addressing these challenges effectively is crucial for a successful partnership and product offering.

From technical perspective, ensuring the partner's product is compatible with the CSP's existing systems, technologies, and platforms. This involves addressing differences in programming languages, APIs, data formats, and protocols to ensure seamless communication and interoperability between systems.

From pricing and billing perspective, complexities arise due to the need to combine different pricing models, billing systems, and customer expectations into a coherent and manageable framework.

Partners may have pricing models that are significantly different from those of the CSP, including subscription-based, usage-based, tiered pricing, or one-time charges. Integrating these models requires flexibility in the CSP's billing system to accommodate and accurately bill for varied pricing structures.

Customers expect a single, consolidated bill for all services, requiring the CSP to integrate the partner's billing data into their own billing systems seamlessly.

The integration often necessitates advanced billing systems capable of handling automated calculations, prorations, discounts, and other billing complexities across different services and pricing models.

7.1.4 Revenue Settlement

A smooth and automated revenue settlement process between a product partner and a Cloud Service Provider (CSP) is crucial for several reasons, affecting not just the operational efficiency and financial health of both parties, but also their strategic relationships and customer satisfaction levels.

Smooth and predictable revenue settlements help both CSPs and their partners manage their cash flows better. Timely settlements ensure that businesses have the necessary funds available for reinvestment, operational costs, and strategic initiatives. This is particularly important for smaller partners who may rely heavily on these payments to maintain their cash flow.

As the business grows, so does the complexity and volume of transactions. An automated and efficient revenue settlement process is scalable, capable of handling increased business without a corresponding increase in overheads or errors. This scalability is crucial for CSPs and their partners to adapt to market demands, customer growth, and the introduction of new products and services seamlessly.

Designing a smooth and automated settlement system between a Cloud Service Provider (CSP) and its product partners requires careful planning, collaboration, and the implementation of robust technology solutions.

Define Clear Agreements

Clearly define the revenue-sharing models and payment structures. This could include fixed fees, percentage shares, tiered pricing, or usage-based models.

Establish SLAs that include settlement timelines, accuracy standards, dispute resolution mechanisms, and penalties for non-compliance.

Agree on the types of data required for settlement, such as usage metrics, customer information, and billing details.

Implement an Integrated Billing Platform

Use billing platforms that support automation in calculating revenues, dues, and settlements. Ensure the platform can handle the agreed-upon revenue-sharing model and adapt to changes in partnership agreements.

The system should seamlessly integrate with both the CSP's and partners' systems for data exchange, ensuring real-time or near-real-time accuracy in billing information.

Establish a Dispute Resolution Framework

Set up automated alerts for discrepancies that exceed predefined thresholds, ensuring timely attention to potential issues.

Define clear procedures for dispute resolution, including escalation paths, timelines, and documentation requirements.

By following these steps, CSPs can design a settlement system that not only automates and streamlines the financial transactions with their product partners but also fosters strong, transparent, and productive partnerships. This approach minimizes administrative burdens, reduces the potential for errors and disputes, and supports scalable and sustainable business growth.

7.1.5 Cloud Marketplace

Cloud Service Providers (CSPs) increasingly recognize the value of having a cloud marketplace as a pivotal component of their strategy. A cloud marketplace serves as a digital platform where customers can discover, purchase, and manage cloud services and applications from various vendors.

Here are some of the key reasons why CSPs need a cloud marketplace:

- **Enhanced Customer Experience**

  A cloud marketplace provides a centralized location where customers can browse, compare, and purchase a variety of cloud services and solutions. This convenience enhances the customer experience by simplifying the process of acquiring cloud technology.

  Customers can manage all their subscriptions and services through a single interface, making it easier to monitor usage, costs, and performance without having to deal with multiple vendors individually.

- **Increased Revenue Opportunities**

  CSPs can leverage the marketplace to promote complementary services or higher-tier plans alongside the primary offerings. For example, a customer purchasing cloud storage might also be shown options for related security services or data analytics tools.

By hosting third-party solutions alongside their own offerings, CSPs can provide a more comprehensive range of products and services, which can attract a wider range of customers.

- **Partner Ecosystem Development**

  A cloud marketplace fosters a vibrant ecosystem of partners whose products and services can integrate with or complement the CSP's offerings. This collaboration can drive innovation and deliver more holistic solutions to customers.

  Overall, a cloud marketplace is not just a sales channel; it's a strategic asset that enhances the CSP's service delivery, expands its reach, builds its brand, and creates a dynamic ecosystem that benefits both the provider and its customers.

7.2 Sales Partner

Cloud Service Providers (CSPs) often collaborate with sales partners to expand their market reach, enhance their service offerings, and achieve various strategic objectives. Sales partners can include resellers, agents, managed service providers, and other entities that can sell or recommend the CSP's services to end customers.

Sales partners can help CSPs access new markets and customer segments that might be difficult to reach directly, either due to geographical, linguistic, or sector-specific barriers. Partners often have established relationships and a deep understanding of their local markets, which can facilitate quicker and more effective market penetration.

Sales partners usually have existing relationships with potential customers, including trust and credibility. By leveraging these relationships, CSPs can more easily gain new customers who might be hesitant to switch services or adopt cloud solutions from an unfamiliar provider.

Therefore, sales partners extend the sales and marketing capabilities of a CSP, contributing additional resources, local market knowledge, and marketing efforts. This collaborative approach can significantly enhance the reach and effectiveness of promotional campaigns and sales initiatives.

For Cloud Service Providers (CSPs), sales partnerships can be categorized into several types based on the nature of the partnership, the role of the partner, and the value they bring to the CSP and its customers. Understanding these different types can help CSPs tailor their partner strategies to best suit their business models and market objectives.

1. Resellers

Resellers purchase cloud services from CSPs and then sell them to their own customers, often adding a markup. They might bundle the CSP's services with their own or with services from other providers to create a comprehensive solution for their clients. Resellers typically handle billing and customer support for the end users.

2. Distributors

Distributors act as intermediaries that facilitate the distribution of cloud services to a wide network of resellers. They often provide added value by offering sales support, marketing resources, and technical training to help resellers successfully market and sell the CSP's services.

3. Managed Service Providers (MSPs)

MSPs offer managed cloud services on top of the infrastructure provided by CSPs. They often provide added services such as managing and operating cloud infrastructure, security services, monitoring, and support on behalf of their clients, offering a more hands-off experience for businesses looking to utilize cloud services.

4. System Integrators (SIs)

System Integrators specialize in creating custom solutions that integrate multiple systems, software, and cloud services into a cohesive IT environment for their clients. SIs work closely with CSPs to ensure that cloud services are seamlessly integrated with existing client systems and workflows.

5. Value-Added Resellers (VARs)

VARs add features or services to the CSP's original cloud offerings and then sell it as an integrated product or complete turn-key solution. This could include additional software, consulting services, custom development, or specific hardware integration.

6. Cloud Brokers

Cloud brokers act as intermediaries that manage the use, performance, and delivery of cloud services, and negotiate relationships between CSPs and their customers. They can help clients choose the right services from multiple CSPs, manage contracts, and ensure that the cloud services are optimized for the client's needs.

7. Affiliate Partners

Affiliate partners promote the CSP's services through various channels (such as blogs, social media, or email marketing) and receive a commission for every customer they refer who signs up for the service. This model is typically less involved than reselling or managing services.

8. Consulting Partners

Consulting partners advise clients on the best ways to leverage cloud services within their business operations, often recommending specific CSPs that fit the client's needs. They may also assist with migration, implementation, and optimization of cloud services.

Each type of sales partner brings different strengths and focuses to the table, and CSPs often engage with multiple types of partners to fully leverage their market reach, technical capabilities, and value-added services. A well-structured partner ecosystem can significantly extend a CSP's market penetration, scalability, and the overall value proposition to end customers.

7.2.1 Reseller & Distributor

The roles of resellers and distributors in the context of Cloud Service Providers (CSPs) have distinct characteristics and functions within the cloud services ecosystem. Understanding these differences is crucial for CSPs to effectively manage their sales channels and for businesses to choose the right partnership model. Here's a breakdown of the primary differences between resellers and distributors:

Resellers

1. **Direct Sales to End Customers**: Resellers typically buy cloud services from CSPs and sell them directly to the end customers. They may target specific markets or industries, leveraging their expertise or customer relationships within those sectors.

2. **Value Addition**: Many resellers add value to the cloud services they sell through bundling with other products or services, providing custom configurations, or offering additional support and consulting services tailored to the needs of their customers.

3. **Customer Relationship**: Resellers often manage the entire customer relationship, including billing, support, and account management. This close relationship with the end customer allows them to offer personalized services and support.

4. **Smaller Scale**: While not always the case, resellers often operate on a smaller scale than distributors, focusing on specific niches or local markets where they can provide tailored solutions and establish strong customer relationships.

Distributors

1. **Channel Management**: Distributors serve as intermediaries between CSPs and a network of resellers or smaller service providers. They do not typically sell directly to the end customer but instead focus on enabling their network of resellers to effectively sell and support cloud services.

2. **Support and Enablement**: Distributors provide value-added services such as training, technical support, marketing assistance, and financial services to their network of resellers. Their role is to empower resellers to succeed in their sales and implementation efforts.

3. **Scale and Reach**: Distributors often operate on a larger scale, working with multiple resellers across broader geographic regions. They have the infrastructure to manage logistics, licensing, and support for a wide range of products and services from multiple CSPs.

4. **Inventory and Logistics Management**: For physical products associated with cloud services (like networking equipment or hardware for hybrid solutions), distributors handle inventory and logistics, ensuring that resellers can fulfill customer orders efficiently.

In summary, resellers focus on selling directly to the end customer, often adding value through customization, bundling, and personalized support. Distributors, on the other hand, act as a bridge between CSPs and a network of resellers, providing the necessary tools, training, and support to enable the resellers to effectively market, sell, and implement cloud solutions. The choice between working with a reseller or a distributor depends on a company's specific needs, scale, and the level of support required.

In the sales ecosystem of Cloud Service Providers (CSP), Resellers and Distributors have distinct positions and primary tasks, yet there is a close collaborative relationship between them. Distributors are typically responsible for channeling products and services from producers to the market, while Resellers directly target end–users, handling product sales and service provision. Given their key role in the ecosystem's supply chain and logistics, Distributors often develop and manage Resellers to broaden market coverage and enhance sales efficiency.

Despite their differing roles, CSPs usually manage these two types of partners within a unified system and process. This approach offers several advantages:

1. **Streamlined Management Processes**: Integrating the management of both types of partners into a single system simplifies internal processes, reducing management costs and operational complexity.

2. **Uniform Standards and Policies**: Ensuring all partners operate according to the same standards and policies helps maintain brand image consistency and ensures a uniform customer experience.

3. **Strengthened Partner Relationships**: Sharing resources, training, and support strengthens relationships with Resellers and Distributors, enhancing their sales capabilities and service levels, thereby driving overall sales growth.

4. **More Efficient Resource Allocation**: A unified management system allows for more efficient allocation of resources. CSPs can adjust support based on market demand and partner performance flexibly, ensuring the effective use of resources.

In the ecosystem of Cloud Service Providers (CSP), resellers and distributors typically represent the most numerous and widely covered types of Sales Partners.

7.2.2 Recruitment & Onboarding

Designing an effective process and management rules for recruiting and onboarding sales partners, such as resellers and distributors, is crucial for a Cloud Service Provider (CSP) to build a successful partner ecosystem.

Clearly define the characteristics and criteria of the ideal sales partners based on factors such as industry expertise, geographic coverage, existing customer base, sales experience, and alignment with the CSP's target market and offerings.

Create a strategic plan for identifying and attracting potential sales partners. This may involve leveraging industry networks, attending trade shows and events, conducting targeted outreach campaigns, and utilizing digital marketing channels.

Develop a structured onboarding process to ensure that newly recruited sales partners understand the CSP's value proposition, products, services, sales processes, and partner program requirements. Provide comprehensive training, documentation, and resources to support their success.

Implementing a self-service onboarding mechanism for resellers and distributors of a CSP (Cloud Service Provider) can streamline the partner enrollment process and empower partners to get started quickly. Here's how to design a self-service onboarding mechanism:

1. **Online Enrollment Portal**: Create an intuitive online portal where potential resellers and distributors can easily access information about the partner program and begin the enrollment process. The portal should provide clear guidance on how to sign up and what information is required for registration.

2. **Self-Registration Form**: Develop a self-registration form that partners can fill out electronically to express their interest in joining the program. Collect essential details such as company information, contact details, industry focus, geographic coverage, and relevant experience.

3. **Document Repository**: Provide access to a document repository or knowledge base where partners can access program guidelines, terms and conditions, training materials, sales resources, and marketing assets. Ensure that documents are organized, searchable, and regularly updated.

4. **Training Modules**: Offer self-paced training modules and certification courses that partners can complete online to

learn about the CSP's products, services, and sales processes. Include quizzes, assessments, and interactive content to reinforce learning and measure comprehension.

5. **Partner Agreement Signing**: Enable partners to electronically sign partnership agreements, contracts, and legal documents within the portal using digital signature technology. Provide clear explanations of the terms and conditions and allow partners to review and accept them electronically.

6. **Automated Approval Process**: Implement an automated approval process that reviews partner applications and verifies eligibility criteria automatically. Use predefined criteria and business rules to determine whether a partner meets the requirements for enrollment.

7. **Notification and Welcome Kit**: Send automated notifications to partners upon successful enrollment, welcoming them to the program and providing instructions on next steps. Deliver a digital welcome kit containing program benefits, onboarding resources, and contact information for support.

8. **Access to Partner Portal**: Grant partners access to a dedicated partner portal where they can manage their account, track their progress, access training materials, register deals, submit support tickets, and communicate with the CSP's partner team.

For sales partners like MSPs (Managed Service Providers), SIs (System Integrators), VARs (Value-Added Resellers), etc., more complex offline communication and personalized collaboration models are typically required. Due to their limited numbers and diverse collaboration models, automated online onboarding may not be suitable. Instead, the following approaches are recommended:

1. **Personalized Contact**: Engage in personalized communication with each potential partner to understand their business needs, collaboration willingness, and expectations. Customize communications through phone calls, meetings, or face-to-face discussions to ensure effective partnerships.

2. **Tailored Solutions**: Customize collaboration plans and schemes based on the specific needs and capabilities of partners. Flexibly adjust collaboration terms, product pricing, support services, etc., to meet partner requirements and facilitate collaboration.

3. **Training and Support**: Provide customized training programs and technical support for partners to familiarize them with CSP products and solutions, enhancing their sales and delivery capabilities. Offer regular training sessions, technical workshops, and expert support to ensure partners are equipped to fulfill their roles.

4. **Collaboration Agreement**: Negotiate collaboration details and terms, and sign collaboration agreements and contracts. Ensure agreements include clear collaboration scopes, responsibilities, compensation mechanisms, and performance evaluation criteria to avoid ambiguity and disputes in future collaborations.

5. **Ongoing Communication**: Establish continuous communication mechanisms to stay closely connected with partners, and regularly review collaboration progress and performance. Promptly address issues, provide support, and

adjust collaboration strategies and plans based on market changes and partner feedback.

6. **Partner Relationship Management**: Establish dedicated partner relationship management teams responsible for managing relationships and business expansion with partners. Through professional partner managers or channel managers, comprehensively handle partner training, support, and business promotion to ensure partner satisfaction and loyalty.

By employing these methods, CSPs can effectively establish close collaboration with MSPs, SIs, VARs, and other sales partners, jointly explore markets, and achieve business growth and mutual success.

7.2.3 Incentive Programs

An incentive program for sales partners of a CSP (Cloud Service Provider) typically involves offering rewards, bonuses, or commissions to motivate and incentivize partners to sell the CSP's products or services. These incentives can vary widely depending on the CSP's goals, the type of products or services being sold, and the performance metrics used to measure partner success.

1. **Commission Structure:** Partners may earn commissions based on the revenue generated from their sales. The commission structure can vary, with partners earning a percentage of the total sale, a flat fee per sale, or a tiered commission structure based on sales volume.

2. **Profit Margin:** For resellers and distributors, the profit model typically involves obtaining a favorable discount from the CSP (Cloud Service Provider) and then reselling the products or services to customers at a different price, thereby earning a profit margin from the price difference.

3. **Sales Targets:** Partners may be given sales targets or quotas to meet in order to qualify for incentives. These targets could be based on revenue, number of sales, or other performance metrics.

4. **Performance Bonuses:** In addition to regular commissions, partners may be eligible for performance bonuses for achieving specific milestones or exceeding sales targets.

5. **Special Promotions:** CSPs may run special promotions or campaigns that offer additional incentives for promoting specific products or services, launching new offerings, or targeting certain market segments.

- **Commission Structure**

A good commission program for sales partners in the cloud industry should be designed to incentivize and reward partners for driving sales, acquiring new customers, and promoting cloud solutions effectively. Here are some key elements to consider when creating such a program:

1. **Competitive Commission Rates:** Offer competitive commission rates that reflect the value of the cloud solutions being sold and the effort required by partners to drive sales. Ensure that the rates are attractive enough to motivate partners while still being financially sustainable for your business.

2. **Tiered Commission Structure:** Implement a tiered commission structure that rewards partners for achieving different levels of performance. Higher sales volumes or reaching specific milestones could result in increased commission rates or additional bonuses, providing extra motivation for partners to excel.

3. **Recurring Revenue Incentives:** Provide incentives for partners to focus on generating recurring revenue streams, such as subscription-based services or renewals. Offering commissions on recurring revenue can help build long-term partnerships and ensure ongoing revenue streams for both partners and the CSP.

4. **New Customer Acquisition Bonuses:** Offer bonuses or enhanced commission rates for partners who bring in new customers to the cloud platform. Acquiring new customers is essential for business growth, and incentivizing partners to focus on this aspect can help expand the customer base effectively.

5. **Product Mix Incentives:** Encourage partners to promote a diverse range of cloud products and services by offering incentives for selling specific product bundles or solutions. This can help drive adoption of new offerings and ensure that partners have a comprehensive understanding of the entire product portfolio.

6. **Transparent and Timely Payments:** Ensure that commission payments are transparent, accurate, and delivered in a timely manner. Clear communication about commission structures, eligibility criteria, and payment processes can help build trust and strengthen relationships with partners.

By incorporating these elements into your commission program for sales partners in the cloud industry, you can create a compelling incentive structure that motivates partners to drive sales, expand the customer base, and contribute to the overall success of your cloud business.

7.2.4 Renewal & Termination

When it comes to the renewal and termination of sales partnerships with CSPs (Cloud Service Providers), several special aspects need to be carefully considered to ensure a smooth and fair process for both parties involved. Some key considerations include:

1. **Contractual Terms**: Review the terms and conditions outlined in the sales partnership agreement regarding renewal and termination clauses. Ensure that both parties understand their rights, obligations, and any notice periods required for renewal or termination.

2. **Performance Evaluation**: Assess the performance of the sales partner based on predefined metrics and key performance indicators (KPIs). Evaluate factors such as sales performance, customer satisfaction, adherence to contractual terms, and overall contribution to business objectives.

3. **Renewal Negotiations**: Initiate renewal discussions well in advance of the contract expiration date. Evaluate the sales partner's performance and discuss any necessary improvements or modifications to the partnership agreement. Negotiate renewal terms, including pricing, incentives, and support resources, to align with both parties' interests.

4. **Termination Procedures**: Establish clear procedures for terminating the sales partnership in the event of non-performance, breach of contract, or other justifiable reasons. Adhere to contractual requirements regarding notice periods, termination fees, and any post-termination obligations or liabilities.

5. **Transition Planning**: Develop a transition plan to facilitate a smooth handover of responsibilities and resources in the

event of partnership termination. Identify alternative sales channels or partners to minimize disruptions to sales activities and customer relationships.

6. **Legal and Compliance Considerations**: Ensure compliance with legal requirements, including labor laws, intellectual property rights, and data protection regulations, when terminating a sales partnership. Seek legal advice to mitigate potential risks and liabilities associated with contract termination.

7. **Communication Strategy**: Communicate openly and transparently with the sales partner throughout the renewal or termination process. Provide clear reasons for any decisions made and offer support or guidance to facilitate a positive outcome.

8. **Relationship Management**: Maintain professional relationships with the sales partner, even in the event of termination, to preserve goodwill and reputation within the industry. Handle disputes or disagreements with tact and diplomacy to minimize negative impacts on business relationships.

By carefully considering these special aspects and following best practices in renewal and termination processes, CSPs can effectively manage their sales partnerships while upholding contractual obligations and maintaining positive business relationships.

Renewal management for sales partners of CSPs (Cloud Service Providers) often requires robust software functionality to streamline processes, track performance, and ensure efficient renewal negotiations. Some key software functions needed for renewal management include:

1. **Contract Management**: Software should allow for centralized storage and management of sales partnership contracts, including renewal terms, expiration dates, and key clauses. This enables easy access to contract details and ensures compliance with renewal deadlines.

2. **Performance Tracking**: Implement tools to track the performance of sales partners against predefined metrics and KPIs. This includes monitoring sales performance, revenue generation, customer satisfaction scores, and adherence to contractual obligations.

3. **Automated Notifications**: Set up automated notifications and reminders to alert stakeholders of upcoming contract renewals and associated deadlines. This helps prevent missed renewal opportunities and ensures timely action.

4. **Renewal Forecasting**: Utilize forecasting capabilities to predict renewal rates and identify opportunities for proactive renewal initiatives. Analyze historical data and trends to anticipate renewal outcomes and plan accordingly.

5. **Negotiation Support**: Provide tools to support renewal negotiations, such as access to historical contract data, pricing models, and incentive structures. Enable collaboration between sales teams and partners to facilitate informed decision-making during negotiations.

6. **Document Generation**: Offer functionality for generating renewal proposals, amendments, and contracts directly within the software platform. Streamline the document creation process and ensure consistency in renewal terms and conditions.

7. **Workflow Automation**: Implement workflow automation to streamline renewal processes, including approval

workflows, document routing, and task assignments. This reduces manual effort, minimizes errors, and accelerates the renewal cycle.

By leveraging these software functions, CSPs can effectively manage the renewal process for sales partners, optimize renewal rates, and strengthen partner relationships while driving business growth.

For the termination of sales partners, similar to renewal, it requires centralized contract data support, automated workflow processes and notifications.

Additionally, when terminating a sales partnership, the transition of existing customers is crucial, as it affects their business continuity and satisfaction. Here are some important details of this process:

1. **Customer Communication:** Notify affected customers in advance of the termination, explaining the reasons and plans. This can be done through formal letters, emails, or phone calls.

2. **Involvement of New Partners:** Identify new partners or internal teams to take over the services and support for existing customers, ensuring they have the capability and resources to meet customer needs.

3. **Customer Training and Support:** Ensure that new partners or teams receive adequate training on customer needs, system configurations, and existing support agreements. They should also establish good relationships with customers and provide ongoing support to ensure business continuity.

4. **Data Migration and System Conversion:** Ensure smooth migration of customer data and system configurations to the platform of the new partner or internal team, ensuring compatibility between systems and seamless integration.

5. **Monitoring and Feedback:** Supervise services and support during the transition period, collect customer feedback, and address any issues promptly while continuously improving service quality.

By implementing the above details, customers can smoothly transition to new service providers after the termination of the sales partnership, ensuring business continuity.

7.3 Service Partner

In the cloud industry, customers can access various professional services to help them successfully migrate to the cloud environment and leverage the benefits of cloud services to the fullest. Here are some common professional services:

- **Solution Consulting:** Providing customized cloud solution consulting services to clients, designing and planning the most suitable cloud architecture and deployment solutions based on their business needs and objectives.

- **Migration and Implementation Services:** Assisting clients in migrating existing applications and data to the cloud platform, including planning migration strategies, executing migration processes, and deploying and configuring cloud services.

- **Operations and Maintenance Services:** Providing 24/7 operational support and management services, including monitoring system performance, troubleshooting, security patching, backup and recovery, ensuring the stable operation of the cloud environment.

- **Optimization Services:** Analyzing and optimizing clients' cloud architectures and applications to improve system efficiency, reliability, and security, optimizing resource utilization and cost-effectiveness.

- **Security and Compliance Services:** Providing security assessments, compliance audits, vulnerability management, and other services to ensure clients' data and applications are adequately protected in the cloud environment and comply with relevant regulations and standards.

- **Training and Education Services:** Offering training courses and educational resources tailored to clients' teams to help them understand and master cloud computing technologies and best practices, enhancing team capabilities and technical skills.

- **Disaster Recovery and Backup Services:** Designing and implementing disaster recovery and backup solutions to ensure clients' business continuity and data security, mitigating the impact of unforeseen events on business operations.

- **Data Management and Analytics Services:** Assisting clients in managing and analyzing large volumes of data, including data storage, backup and recovery, data analysis, and visualization services, providing data-driven insights and decision support.

These professional services can help clients leverage the advantages of cloud computing, address business challenges, and enhance efficiency and competitiveness.

In the cloud industry, not all of these services are necessarily provided directly by the Cloud Service Provider (CSP). On the contrary, CSPs often collaborate with service partners, who deliver these services to end customers on behalf of the CSP.

These service partners may specialize in specific areas or offer a comprehensive suite of services, depending on their expertise and capabilities. By partnering with these service providers, CSPs can extend their service offerings, leverage the partners' specialized skills and resources, and provide a broader range of solutions to meet the diverse needs of their customers.

Service partners play a crucial role in the ecosystem, serving as an extension of the CSP's capabilities and helping customers navigate their cloud journey more effectively. They bring domain expertise, technical proficiency, and industry experience to the table, enhancing the overall value proposition for customers and driving adoption of cloud services.

7.3.1 Solution Consulting Partner

For a Cloud Solution Provider (CSP) that is just starting up, selecting the right type of service partner is crucial for initial market penetration and development. In this early stage, partnering with a solution consulting firm can be particularly advantageous. A solution consulting partner specializes in crafting comprehensive solutions that cater specifically to the unique needs of customers. This not only ensures that the CSP's offerings are adequately tailored but also facilitates effective product promotion.

Consulting partners excel in analyzing a customer's specific business needs and then crafting solutions that integrate the CSP's technologies to solve those needs. This personalized approach helps in demonstrating the direct value of the CSP's products to potential clients.

These partners typically bring in-depth knowledge of various industries and can guide CSPs in targeting the right market segments and customer bases. Their expertise helps in navigating complex market dynamics and in positioning the CSP's offerings effectively.

By aligning with reputable consultants, a new CSP can leverage the established credibility and existing customer relationships of its partners. This is particularly valuable for a new entrant in the competitive cloud services market.

Working closely with a consulting partner provides a CSP with valuable feedback on its offerings directly from the market, enabling rapid adjustments and improvements to better meet customer expectations.

As the CSP grows, the role of the consulting partner may evolve from providing market entry support to assisting with scaling operations, diversifying product lines, or even going international. The flexibility and adaptability of both parties in this partnership can significantly influence the success and growth trajectory of the CSP.

7.3.2 Managed Service Partner

In the cloud industry, managed services refer to the outsourcing of daily IT management for cloud-based services and technical support to automate and enhance the business operations. Often, this service is provided by managed service providers (MSPs) who manage and assume responsibility for providing a defined set of services to their clients either proactively or as they (the MSP) determine that services are needed. Managed cloud services can include everything from cloud deployment, management, monitoring, and optimization to security and compliance support.

Key Components of Managed Cloud Services

1. Cloud Deployment and Management: This includes setting up and managing the cloud infrastructure. MSPs handle the deployment of applications across cloud environments—be it public, private, or hybrid.

2. Performance Monitoring: Continuous monitoring of the cloud environment to ensure optimal performance. This includes tracking the performance of applications, managing resource allocation, and optimizing load balancing.

3. Security and Compliance: Implementing robust security measures such as identity and access management, threat detection, and data encryption. MSPs also ensure compliance with various regulatory standards like GDPR, HIPAA, or PCI DSS, depending on the client's industry requirements.

4. Data Backup and Recovery: Providing automated data backup solutions and ensuring timely recovery of data in the event of data loss, corruption, or a security breach.

5. Scalability and Flexibility: Managing the scalability of the cloud environment to handle varying workloads and facilitating seamless integration with existing IT resources.

6. Cost Management and Optimization: Helping clients control and optimize their cloud spend by monitoring resource usage and recommending more cost-effective solutions or configurations.

7. Technical Support: Offering ongoing technical support and troubleshooting, often on a 24/7 basis, to resolve issues swiftly and maintain business continuity.

When a Cloud Service Provider (CSP) is selecting a Managed Service Provider (MSP) as a partner, several critical aspects need to be considered to ensure that the partnership is successful and beneficial for both parties, as well as for the end customers. Here are the key points CSPs should pay attention to:

Technical Alignment and Expertise

Ensure the MSP has expertise in the technologies and platforms your services are based on.

Assess the MSP's proficiency with cloud environments, particularly if they hold any specializations or certifications relevant to your technology stack.

Security and Compliance

Check that the MSP has robust security measures in place to protect data integrity, confidentiality, and availability.

The MSP must adhere to the industry-specific compliance requirements that are relevant to your customers, such as HIPAA for healthcare or GDPR for European data protection.

Service Level Agreements (SLAs)

Examine the MSP's SLAs to ensure they match or exceed the performance and uptime guarantees you promise to your clients.

Ensure the MSP can provide rapid responses and resolutions as per the agreed SLAs, which is crucial for maintaining customer satisfaction.

Evaluate the quality of support the MSP provides, including the availability of support (24/7, business hours, etc.), the channels of support (phone, email, live chat), and the languages supported. Look at customer testimonials and feedback to gauge the MSP's reputation in handling customer issues and their commitment to customer satisfaction.

Geographical Coverage

If geographic proximity is important for service delivery or compliance, ensure the MSP has a presence in the necessary locations.

For CSPs with a global clientele, an MSP with multi-region capabilities and knowledge of local regulations is crucial.

Selecting the right MSP involves a detailed evaluation of these factors. By aligning on these critical points, a CSP can ensure that their managed service partner will effectively contribute to providing high-quality, secure, and scalable services to their customers.

7.3.3 Service as Sales

In the cloud industry, a service partner can act as a sales partner by playing an integral role in expanding the market reach and sales capabilities of a Cloud Service Provider (CSP). Here's how this relationship typically works and benefits both parties:

Lead Generation and Customer Acquisition

Service partners often have their own customer bases and can refer these clients to the CSP when additional or complementary cloud services are required. This referral system is a direct route to new customer leads.

By participating in joint marketing efforts, such as co-branded events, webinars, and case studies, service partners help to raise awareness and generate leads in sectors where they already have a strong presence.

Sales Enablement

Service partners can bundle their services with cloud offerings. For example, an MSP might offer a package that includes both cloud infrastructure and ongoing management services, making it easier for customers to adopt the solution.

Through their ongoing relationships and deep understanding of their customers' businesses, service partners can identify opportunities to introduce additional cloud services that address evolving needs, effectively upselling or cross-selling the CSP's offerings.

Customer Education and Demonstrations

Service partners often conduct training sessions and workshops to educate potential customers about the benefits of cloud services, how to use them effectively, and the specific advantages of their partnered CSP's offerings.

They can demonstrate the CSP's products in action, showcasing real-world applications and benefits to potential customers, which can help in convincing them to choose the CSP's solutions.

Contracting and Negotiations

Service partners can assist in negotiating and closing complex deals by addressing specific customer concerns, leveraging their established relationships, and understanding of the customer's business environment.

Customer Retention and Renewal

Service partners maintain ongoing relationships with customers, providing them with regular updates and insights into their cloud services, which helps in renewing and retaining customer contracts.

The concept of "service as sales," where excellent customer service is leveraged as a primary driver for sales, is increasingly significant in many industries, including the cloud industry. This approach reflects a shift from traditional sales methods towards a more integrated and customer-focused strategy.

Service-focused sales strategies emphasize building strong relationships with customers. By prioritizing customer needs and providing high-quality service, businesses can build trust and loyalty. This trust is crucial for repeat business and long-term retention.

In industries where products and prices are often similar, outstanding service can differentiate one company from another. This differentiation is vital in the cloud industry, where customers may struggle to distinguish between the myriad of available options based solely on technical specifications or pricing.

Therefore, Cloud Service Providers (CSPs) must carefully design business models with service partners that go beyond mere service outsourcing, aiming to create synergistic relationships that empower these partners to actively sell and promote products. This approach can significantly amplify a CSP's reach and effectiveness in the market. Here are several key elements to consider when designing such a business model:

- **Partner Incentivization and Rewards**

Implement clear and attractive commission structures that reward service partners for not only servicing clients but also for actively selling products. This could include tiered commission rates that increase with sales volume or the complexity of deals closed.

Offer additional incentives for achieving specific targets, such as new customer acquisition, high customer satisfaction scores, or successful deployment of complex solutions.

- **Integrated Sales and Service Training**

Ensure that service partners have thorough knowledge and understanding of the CSP's product offerings through regular training sessions. This includes updates on new features, benefits, and potential use cases.

Provide sales training that equips partners with effective sales techniques and strategies tailored to the cloud market. This should also cover consultative selling skills, which are crucial for understanding and addressing customer needs effectively.

- **Joint Marketing Efforts**

Develop marketing materials and campaigns that co-brand the services and products, presenting the CSP and the service partner as aligned entities. This can enhance the market presence and credibility of both.

Share the costs of marketing efforts, making it easier for service partners to engage in promotional activities. This can include digital marketing, events, and trade shows.

- **Empowerment through Data Sharing**

Give partners access to analytics and performance reporting tools that can help them understand customer behaviors, product performance, and market trends. Empowered with data, partners can more effectively sell and tailor their approaches to meet customer needs.

Share insights about customer usage patterns, satisfaction levels, and service metrics that can help partners optimize their sales strategies and improve service delivery.

By designing a business model that closely integrates service partners into both the sales and operational aspects of the business, CSPs can create a powerful network that drives growth, enhances service delivery, and improves customer satisfaction across the board. This partnership strategy not only expands the sales force but also deepens the market penetration and adaptability of the CSP.

8

BUSINESS EXCELLENCE IN TECHNOLOGY INDUSTRY

James Watt was not the inventor of the steam engine, but the one who enhanced it and effectively promoted its wide application. The first steam engine was invented by Thomas Newcomen in 1712, mainly for pumping water out of coal mines. Although Newcomen's engine solved the problem of mine drainage, it was very inefficient, with a large amount of steam energy wasted in the process of cooling and reheating.

Watt's contribution was in his significant technical improvements to the steam engine. In 1765, he introduced a separate condenser, greatly increasing the efficiency of the engine. This improvement enabled the steam engine to be used not only for pumping water but also in other industrial sectors, such as textiles, metallurgy, and transportation, thus triggering the wave of the Industrial Revolution.

Watt not only had technical insight but also a keen understanding of how to align technology with market demands. He collaborated with businessman Matthew Boulton to form the Boulton & Watt company, which promoted and expanded the use of steam engines in various industries. They not only provided steam engines but also offered after-sales services to help users optimize their operations, a key factor in their commercial success.

Watt's success was not only about technological innovation but also his ability to commercialize his inventions and his acute understanding of market needs. Therefore, Watt is known as the "improver" of the steam engine rather than its inventor, because he transformed it from a simple mine drainage device into a key driver of industrial power, ultimately making it a force that changed the world.

Thomas Edison played a vital role in the promotion of electricity, even though he was not the inventor of electrical technology. Research on electricity had begun long before him, with scientists such as Michael Faraday and James Clerk Maxwell laying the theoretical foundation for electrical technology. However, Thomas Edison's contribution was in converting electricity from a laboratory phenomenon into a practical and widely applicable technology, ultimately ushering in the modern electrical era.

One of Edison's key contributions was the invention of the incandescent light bulb. While he was not the first to invent the light bulb, he created the first truly economical and long-lasting electric bulb. His version was more efficient and cheaper to produce, making electric lighting affordable for ordinary households and businesses.

Edison's true success, however, lay in his promotion of the entire electrical system. He didn't just invent the light bulb; he also designed and developed a complete electrical distribution network, which included generators, distribution systems, and switching devices. In 1882, he built the world's first commercial power station, the Pearl Street Station in New York City, which supplied electricity to nearby homes and businesses, marking the beginning of large-scale electrical use.

Edison's marketing strategy was also crucial. He promoted direct current (DC) electrical networks and vigorously publicized the advantages of his technology in both public and media circles. Although DC was eventually replaced by alternating current (AC), championed by Nikola Tesla and George Westinghouse, Edison's contribution was proving that electricity could be commercialized on a large scale and establishing the first commercial electrical system.

Beyond technological innovation, Edison's success was also due to his sharp business acumen and execution skills. He founded General Electric, which is now one of the world's largest electrical companies and became a major platform for the widespread adoption of electrical technology.

In summary, Edison's success was not only due to his improvements to the light bulb but also his establishment of a complete electrical distribution system that brought electricity out of the realm of scientific experiments and into the daily lives of the general public, truly ushering in the electrical age. As mentioned, he possessed both technical understanding and the ability to align technology with market demands, driving the widespread adoption and application of his innovations.

The core competitiveness of the technology industry undoubtedly comes from continuous innovation and a persistent curiosity and pursuit of new things. However, the technologies that have truly transformed human life throughout history did not rely solely on pure technical breakthroughs. Instead, they were driven by pioneers who could seamlessly combine technological innovation with market demand. It is those who have both deep technical knowledge and sharp business acumen that make large-scale application and adoption of these technologies possible.

Whether it was the steam engine during the Industrial Revolution, the electrical systems of the electric age, or modern innovations like computers, the internet, and artificial intelligence, behind them all were individuals with cross-disciplinary abilities. Watt's enhancements to the steam engine transformed it from a mine drainage tool into a key driver of industrial development. Edison not only invented the affordable and practical incandescent light bulb but also established the world's first power distribution system, making electricity a part of everyday life for the masses.

The reason these technologies could leave the confines of the laboratory and reach millions of homes is because there were individuals who could delve deeply into the essence of technology and understand how to align it with market needs. They were not just inventors but also entrepreneurs and strategists. Their success lay in turning complex technological advancements into products and services that the general public could readily accept, thereby advancing society.

Thus, technological progress requires not only scientific breakthroughs and innovations but also leaders who can seize the opportunities of the times, accurately assess market demand, and commercialize these technologies. Only when technology and the market perfectly align can innovation truly change the world.